The media's watching Vault! Here's a sampling of our coverage.

"For those hoping to climb the ladder of success, [Vault's] insights are priceless."
– ***Money magazine***

"The best place on the web to prepare for a job search."
– ***Fortune***

"[Vault guides] make for excellent starting points for job hunters and should be purchased by academic libraries for their career sections [and] university career centers."
– ***Library Journal***

"The granddaddy of worker sites."
– ***US News and World Report***

"A killer app."
– ***New York Times***

One of Forbes' 33 "Favorite Sites"
– ***Forbes***

"To get the unvarnished scoop, check out Vault."
– ***Smart Money Magazine***

"Vault has a wealth of information about major employers and job-searching strategies as well as comments from workers about their experiences at specific companies."
– ***The Washington Post***

"A key reference for those who want to know what it takes to get hired by a law firm and what to expect once they get there."
– ***New York Law Journal***

"Vault [provides] the skinny on working conditions at all kinds of companies from current and former employees."
– ***USA Today***

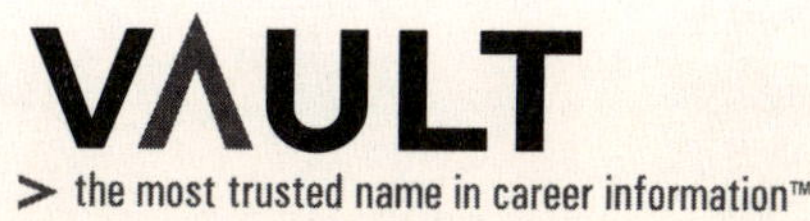

VAULT CAREER GUIDE TO ADVERTISING

VAULT CAREER GUIDE TO ADVERTISING

IRA BERKOWITZ
AND THE STAFF OF VAULT

Library of Congress CIP Data is available.

ISBN 1-58131-267-9

Printed in the United States of America

ACKNOWLEDGEMENTS

Ira Berkowitz's acknowledgments:

My thanks for the valuable insights provided by everyone who helped in the preparation of this book. I am especially grateful to Chuck Bachrach, a giant in the business, and Eric Ober without whose help this book would not have been possible. And, as always, my wife Phyllis for reading the manuscript and smoothing out the rough spots.

Vault's acknowledgments:

Thanks to everyone who had a hand in making this book possible, especially Marcy Lerner, Elena Boldeskou and Kelly Shore. We are also extremely grateful to Vault's entire staff of writers, editors and interns for all their help in the editorial and production processes. Special thanks to Gabrielle Dudnyk for her keen eye.

Vault also would like to acknowledge the support of Matt Doull, Ahmad Al-Khaled, Lee Black, Eric Ober, Hollinger Ventures, Tekbanc, New York City Investment Fund, Globix, Hoover's, Glenn Fischer, Mark Hernandez, Ravi Mhatre, Carter Weiss, Ken Cron, Ed Somekh, Isidore Mayrock, Zahi Khouri, Sana Sabbagh, and other Vault investors, as well as our family and friends.

Table of Contents

Chapter 4: Creating a Campaign 45

Chapter 5: Professional Profiles 53

GETTING HIRED 61

Chapter 6: Advertising Job Search Basics 63

Chapter 7: Resumes, Cover Letters, Interviews and Portfolios 75

APPENDIX 85

Introduction

The concept of advertising existed long before we had a term for it. In 981A.D. the great Viking explorer Eric the Red left Norway to survey an island west of Iceland. Except for the southern coast this new land was little more than a gigantic iceberg. But Eric was a natural at advertising. To persuade immigrants to leave Norway and settle the island, he painted a picture of temperate climate, rolling meadows and lush farmland. To top it all off, he named it Greenland. Eric created a brand. Hundreds of land-starved Vikings boarded longships and headed west for this so-called "greenland."

Advertising is defined as the art of positioning and creating brands and persuading consumers to buy them through messages in mass media. The clothes you wear, the cars you drive, the food you eat and the soft drinks you consume are all brands.

Advertising is a creative and inclusive field unique in the business world. "Advertising agencies are idea stores, and just about everyone gets in on the act," says Chuck Bachrach, media director of the Los Angeles-based full-service advertising agency Rubin Postaer and Associates. "If you have a fire in your belly and want to work with smart, creative, fun people in a business that's virtually blind to race and gender, there's no business quite as satisfying."

At the same time, advertising is a field that's often glamorized – and misunderstood. Read on to understand more about this fascinating industry.

A Guide to this Guide

The *Vault Career Guide to Advertising* is a "how-to" guide with tips and practical information to help you find the advertising job that you want. The book is divided into five sections.

The Scoop: You'll learn about how the advertising industry began, the state of the industry, the outlook for the future, new trends, how an advertising campaign is created, and much more.

On The Job: Provides a realistic look at a day in the life of account services, media and creative, how much the jobs pay, and how to get promoted.

Getting Hired: The section contains valuable information on how to prepare for an advertising career while in school, how to shine during the interview, tips on questions that you will be asked (and how to answer them) and questions you should ask, how to prepare a creative portfolio, the value of internships, how and where to network, creating a killer resume and how to get in the door.

THE SCOOP

- EMBLAZON

Advertising Basics: Branding, History and Trends

CHAPTER 1

Branding

What exactly is a brand? What's the difference between a brand and a product?

David Ogilvy, founder of Ogilvy & Mather, knew something about brands, having created icons like The American Express Card and Rolls Royce. He defined a brand as: "The intangible sum of a product's attributes: its name, packaging, and price, its history, its reputation and the way it's advertised." The best way to understand a brand is to think of it as a friend. We choose brands in exactly the same way we choose friends. Brands are friends; products are strangers. Branding is an emotional process of involvement.

At its most basic level advertising, like friendship, is a three-stage process – awareness, trial and repeat. In the first stage, awareness, you hear about a brand. In the second stage, trial, you're persuaded to buy it and try it. If you like it, you buy it again and again. You're a repeat customer. Along the way, you find that you and the brand share the same values. You wouldn't think about using anything else.

A brand is an image, a conception in consumers' minds. Implicit within the image is a unique promise of value and trust that distinguishes it from its competitors. The job of an advertising agency is to use every tool at its disposal to clothe the brand with substance and endow it with personality – to make it a trusted friend.

Branding and Values

Advertisements are primarily concerned with creating, revamping and promoting brands. But what is a brand? The most basic way to think of a brand is how it is defined on a ranch – as a physical mark placed on cattle that clearly identifies to whom the cattle belong. When the rancher sells the cattle, it also tells the buyers at the cattle market where the cattle came from. We see brands the same way when we take a walk down the grocery aisle, stop in at a fast-food restaurant, buy an expensive pair of shoes. The most effective brands do more than tell us where a product came from. They communicate a brand value, which is how the target market perceives the brand and what attributes they assign to it. These attributes can range from "high-quality," in the case of Burberry, to "reliable" (Volvo) to "very inexpensive" (Wal-Mart). When developing your own brand, you choose to assign attributes to it such as "hard-working" or "culturally aware." When you market that brand, you create a message that communicates to your target market (potential employers, in this case) those attributes you want them to remember.

Involvement and branding go hand in hand. Involvement narrows the gap between product and customers by engaging and involving them in the emotional or intellectual experience of the brand.

Involvement is based on the simple proposition that the closer advertisers get to their customers and, correspondingly, the closer prospective customers get to the brand, the chances of selling them and keeping them increase dramatically.

Advertisers and marketers spend vast amounts of money building new brands or revamping preexisting ones. They first start with a product, a function and a name. They then – and this is the tricky part – develop and refine the more abstract qualities of customer perception, reputation and trust. Yes, customers do buy products and services for sheer functionality, but purchasing decisions go far beyond that.

Consumers also buy things and services that reflect a brand reputation and fit with their own personal values and aspirations. They may develop an emotional relationship with a brand, buying it for the simple reason that they have always bought it, or because it reminds them of their childhood, or because it gives them a taste of the glamour they want in their life. Good advertisers can tap into this well of emotion – and it's a maxim of advertising when products are similar, the advertising has to rely on the difference in the experience. Advertising attaches value to the product by creating the anticipation of a superior experience. (Just take a look, for example, at the Herbal Essences shampoo television ads, which strongly imply that women will be brought to the heights of ecstasy merely by shampooing their hair with the product.)

If the links between customer and brand are properly built, leveraged and translated into an emotionally involving and gratifying experience, an intensely loyal, committed customer will result. Virtually every business follows some variation of the "20/80 rule." Roughly, 20 percent of customers generate 80 percent of sales. Their lifetime value to the brand is significant. The best customers often become brand advocates and recruit new customers.

What Can Be Branded?

It's important to realize that the brand in question might not, in fact, be a traditional product – it might be a place or an experience. For example, John Osborn, executive vice president of integrated marketing at BBDO, led BBDO's efforts on behalf of the "New York Miracle" advertising campaign. The objective of the campaign was to revive tourism over the holiday season following 9/11. The campaign consisted of six television spots featuring famous New Yorkers, such as Woody Allen, Robert DeNiro and Barbara Walters, etc., in a variety of humorous situations. For example, in one spot Woody Allen ice skated at Rockefeller Center, and in another Barbara Walters pretends to audition for a Broadway musical.

At the same time, the consumer has become more cynical and savvy to traditional advertising gambits. Institutions, from the presidency to churches to everyday brands, are no longer instinctively trusted. The increasing saturation of advertising messages – before feature films, on mini-billboards in bathroom stalls and grocery carts – may be causing consumers to tune out most advertising altogether.

As consumers become more finicky, the importance of integrated marketing rises. All aspects of marketing communications (advertising, sales promotion, public relations, and direct marketing) work together as a unified force rather than each working in isolation. A successful campaign means every customer contact with the brand must reinforce and extend its basic message. The look, feel and tone all must convey the essential brand image. The basic proposition of integrated marketing is to surround customers with the brand.

Branding Case: The Volkswagen Beetle

In 1959, Volkswagen assigned its advertising to Doyle Dane Bernbach, then a relatively small New York agency. Its job was daunting. How do you sell a small, bulbous car originally commissioned by Adolph Hitler and looked like a bug to Americans for whom the Second World War was a recent memory? The folks at Doyle Dane Bernbach did it with honesty, quirkiness, and wit. While Detroit carmakers were courting obsolescence by tacking fins on their gigantic cars every year, Volkswagen maintained the car's undersized, rotund shape wile improving performance and keeping the price low. And, in a radical departure for a carmaker, Volkswagen confessed that the car was ugly. They named it the Beetle, turning a liability into an advantage. The car-buying public was charmed. Ads like "Think Small," selected by *Advertising Age* as the top advertising campaign of all time, and "It's Ugly But It Gets You There," propelled sales of Volkswagen through the roof. The advertising was distinctive and resonated with car buyers. Buyers felt smart for looking past the car's supposedly unappealing looks and relished the cost savings.

Another way to reach today's cynical audience is through charm. Especially humorous or clever campaigns can cut through advertising clutter. The much-admired "Joe Isuzu" campaign, which ran from 1986-1990, acknowledged to viewers that car salesmen were often dishonest. Joe would tell enormous lies about Isuzu products, such as claiming that the cars had "more seats than the Astrodome." Occasional subtitles would humorously alert the viewing audience that Joe Isuzu was lying. The campaign flattered and amused viewers enough to make them watch the ads (and made Joe Isuzu a minor celebrity). Other clever forms of advertising may appeal to consumers – such as stickers on mangos in grocery stores inviting the mango purchaser to try Snapple's new mango iced tea. Nostalgia also works – that's why the "Hey, Mikey likes it!" commercial for Life still runs.

Branding Case: Marlboro

Marlboro was a cigarette barely distinguishable from its competitors until Leo Burnett created the Marlboro Man and turned the brand into the best selling cigarette in the world. Back in the 1950s there were no ethical or health problems with cigarettes. But Philip Morris still had a problem – an advertising problem. The company wanted to reposition Marlboro from a women's cigarette to appeal to a much broader audience. The Marlboro Man riding his horse through Marlboro country fit the bill. After introducing the Marlboro Man, sales immediately soared to $5 billion, dwarfing pre-cowboy sales. The advertising was less about smoking than a longed for lifestyle. Freshness and taste were explicitly associated with the great outdoors, a place of soaring mountains, thick forests and, most importantly, rugged individualism. Men, enjoying the fantasy of seeing themselves as rugged, handsome outdoorsy cowboys instead of pasty, black-lunged urbanites, purchased the brand in staggering numbers. Sales promotion was overlaid onto advertising to reinforce the brand image, and the Marlboro Store was opened. For proofs of purchase and a small sum of money, Marlboro smokers could buy premiums (e.g., clothes, lighters, etc.) and involve themselves in the Marlboro experience. Now, the mere reference to a saddle and a hint of red in Marlboro's sales literature still evokes the appealing rustic yet nicotine-laced aura of Marlboro Country.

Media Options

Once an advertising campaign is constructed, it needs to be, well, advertised. Here are the primary conduits for advertising.

Television

Network television: A network is any group of local television stations electronically joined to broadcast the same program at the same time. Network TV is essential for advertising national brands and reaches an audience of 99 percent of U.S. TV households. It offers advertisers a large choice of programs, each with their own demographics, ranging from Saturday morning children's shows to news and sports, to soap operas and prime time shows.

Spot television: Spot television is the purchase of advertising time on a market-by-market basis. Perhaps a brand has only recently entered a new geographic market and needs an advertising branding push only in that location. Or maybe the brand is only available or distributed in a select number of markets (e.g, In-n-out Burgers, a fast-food chain, is only located in California, Nevada and Arizona). In such cases, spot television makes sense. Additionally, buys can incorporate specific market characteristics. For example, viewing levels increase in cold weather markets during the winter, as Northerners cuddle in front of the cozy electronic hearth that is the television set.

Cable television: Introduced in 1960 to improve reception in remote areas, cable television now rivals the networks for audience. According to a lead researcher at Viacom, almost 84 percent of all television homes receive cable – that's 91 million homes! Cable TV provides advertisers with fairly precise demographic, psychographic and geographic targeting, and a more affluent audience than broadcast television because it only exists in households that can afford it. (Demographics are a basic, objective descriptive classification of consumers, such as their age, sex, income, education, size of household, ownership of home and so on.) Most cable TV channels are programmed for narrowcasting – attracting a specific demographic or interest. ESPN is all sports all the time. Animal Planet is designed for animal lovers. AMC aims for aficionados of old movies. If there's an interest with a sufficient audience, you can bet there is or will be a cable channel devoted to it, and advertisers wanting to reach that audience. Cable programs don't attract as many viewers, but wasted audience – those who fall outside of the demographic or interest group – is minimal.

Print advertising

There are three types of print advertising media – consumer magazines, trade magazines and national and local newspapers.

Magazines have a great deal to offer advertisers, with ads that have a long shelf life. Unlike with TV, readers take their time with a magazine. They refer back to it from time to time, increasing ad exposure opportunities, and they can, and often do, pass magazines on to friends and relatives.

Consumer magazines: In these publications, the editorial content appeals to the general public or a specific segment of the public. Educated and affluent consumers tend to be heavy magazine readers and light TV viewers. Consumer magazines offer audience selectivity. They can deliver a defined segment with a minimum of "wasted" (nontargeted) delivery. There are entire magazines devoted to particular subjects (e.g., *Road & Track*, *Golf Digest*, and so on). Magazines also sometimes offer regular features devoted to particular subjects that interest advertisers. For example, *The New Yorker* may offer an issue with a special travel section. Airlines, car rental companies and hotel advertisers in the featured area use the issue to target consumers.

There is an adage in the advertising industry: "The more you tell, the more you sell." Magazines offer room for long, detailed copy and are the perfect environments for products, like drugs or electronic devices, that require extended explanations.

Trade magazines: Aimed at professionals in a particular industry, these magazines are typically not carried on mainstream newsstands, though there are exceptions, such as *Variety* (for media industry insiders.)

Newspapers: People get involved with what affects them personally – in their neighborhoods, at their workplace – and newspapers give them that local information more than any other media vehicle. Smart media buyers leverage these opportunities. Sections like these are replete with ads. Typical newspaper readers are college-educated, in their mid-forties, and a very attractive audience to automotive, electronics and travel advertisers. National newspapers like *The Wall Street Journal* and *USA Today*, and local papers like the *San Francisco Chronicle* or the *Washington Post*, offer a variety of advantages to advertisers. Newspapers are a perfect medium for limited time offers and new product announcements. They underscore the axiom that all advertising is local. Research shows that an ad in the *Charlotte Observer* that mentions Charlotte in the headline will attract more attention than an otherwise identical ad that omits the name of the city in the headline. And, just as in magazines, there is plenty of room for long, detailed copy required for technically oriented brands, like high performance automobiles.

Radio

Radio can be a useful part of a media plan. Like television, radio (AM & FM) is divided into network and spot (local). And like cable TV, it's narrowcasted – it offers stations that play music in virtually every flavor, talk shows, sports programs and news channels. But unlike its broadcast sibling, radio only offers sound, so you can't see the product. In addition, consumers often listen to the radio when they are driving or away from their homes, so they may not absorb the information as readily.

But radio also is much less expensive than TV. Its single dimension – sound – forces copywriters to stimulate the listener's imagination. The average radio station plays up to twenty radio commercials in an hour. In order to break through the "wallpaper" of background noise, intrusive delivery is everything. Music, pacing, humor, audio mnemonic devices – the Green Giant's "Ho, ho, ho", for example – are employed to capture the listeners attention. Some advertisers even use the weather to their advantage. Coca-Cola and other soft drink marketers have issued standing orders for commercials to be played when the temperature reaches 90 degrees. In a media plan, radio ads can target audiences at a relatively low cost. It's also a good way to "surround" consumers with a brand; not as effective by itself, but useful as a way to increase brand recognition and affection.

Out-of-Home

Out-of-home advertising ranges from billboards to bus signs to kiosks to spectacular signs in Times Square. It's used not to build but to reinforce an ad campaign. Only one copy point, or benefit, can be registered.

Surrounding Consumers With the Brand Message - Reach and Frequency

A vital step in a media campaign is the blending of the media forms. Advertising effectiveness often boils down to reach and frequency. Reach is defined as the estimated number of different individuals in the audience reached who experience at least one message during a specific period of time, usually four weeks. Frequency is the number of times you reach them during the same period of time. Typically, the objective is to reach the greatest number of different people several times during the four-week period to aid recall. Television delivers the highest reach of any medium.

But it's not as simple as that. People have short memories. That's when frequency comes into play. Although it delivers broad reach, television time is very expensive, and other less expensive options are often used to generate frequency if money is a concern. (Ubiquitous Nike, for example, spends upwards of $600 million a year on its "Just Do It" advertising.) Because of relatively low out-of-pocket costs, radio and cable can be excellent frequency builders. In many markets, radio spots can be purchased for less than $100 each. Planners look at the array of media options available to them and set reach and frequency objectives to determine the most effective and efficient way to surround consumers with the brand message within the goals and budget of the campaign.

Advertising History

There have been four pivotal inventions that have shaped the media and thus the advertising industry – the printing press, radio, television and the Internet.

The printing press made possible the wide dissemination of information with words on paper, handbills at first, then advertisements in newspapers and magazines. Selling material had to be created and advertising agencies were born. The first advertising agency, Volney B. Palmer, opened in Philadelphia in 1841. By 1861 there were 20 advertising agencies in New York City alone. Among them was J. Walter Thompson, today the oldest American advertising agency in continuous existence.

Radio became a commercial medium in the 1920s. For the first time, advertising could be heard, not just seen. Soap operas, music, and serial adventures populated the new medium, and as radios appeared in virtually every home in America, sales of products advertised on the air soared. Advertisers rushed to write infectious advertising jingles, an art form that still has its place in the advertising repertoire of today.

Then television changed everything. Although TV was invented in the 1920s, it didn't become a mass commercial medium until the 1950s when the prices of television sets began to approach affordability. Print and radio had to take a back seat because, for the first time, commercials were broadcast with sight, sound and motion. The effect on the industry and the way products were sold was remarkable. Advertising agencies not only had to learn how to produce these minimovies in units of 30 and 60 seconds, they had to learn to effectively segment the audience and deliver the right commercial message to the right group of consumers.

Cable television was the next great innovation, offering a greater variety of channels with more specific program offerings. That allowed advertisers to narrowcast. Before the advent of cable television, the networks attempted to reach demographics by airing at different times throughout the broadcast period. Soap operas were broadcast during the day to reach women, news in the evening to reach an older target audience, and sitcoms like *Three's Company* and *Mork and Mindy* to reach specific demographics like men and women in the 18-34 age group during prime time. Cable television, on the other hand, brought with it channels like MTV that catered to young music lovers, ESPN, for (typically) male sports fans, and the Food Network, for people who love cooking (or at least love to watch others cook). These new advertising channels were delightful for advertisers who wished to target certain audiences with specific interests – though less so for the networks, who saw their share of ad revenue dwindle.

The new innovation that's revolutionized advertising? The Internet. What began as an information-sharing tool quickly became a playground for advertising as ad pros took advantage of the new medium to communicate with customers in direct and innovative ways. In the 1990s, advertisers and their agencies hashed out methods of profitably navigating the Internet with its strange assortment of commercial messages. Banners, pop-ups and hot links replaced 30-second commercials and four-color page ads. Interactive agencies, experts at marketing on the Web, became an essential part of agencies' portfolio of services. But there were too many entrants into this nascent field – and too many Web companies based on nothing more than a dream, a foozball table and some overvalued stock. The dot-com collapse in 2000 took out many Web-based companies – and Web-based ad agencies.

Still, the Internet remains a uniquely effective medium for direct and informal communication with consumers. Will the Web continue to grow as an advertising medium? Fortune telling is a risky business, but, as the Magic 8-Ball might say, signs point to yes. According to a recent report by Jupiter Research, online consumer advertising is expected grow to over $7 billion in 2004. Online business-to-business advertising is on the upswing, with expenditures reaching $3.3 billion in the first half of 2003 (that's a 10.5 percent increase over the first half of 2002) according to the Interactive Advertising Bureau and PricewaterhouseCoopers.

The Web has revolutionized the way we shop, book travel, get information and look for jobs, making it an exceptionally fertile ground for consumerism – and advertising. Jupiter Research reports that e-commerce sales to consumers will reach $65 billion in 2004, a 24 percent increase over 2003. While that represents a mere 3 percent of total retail sales, that percentage represents remarkable growth. In addition, interactive media advertisers indicate that the field is expanding in part because of an influx of "traditional" advertisers into the field, like McDonald's and Frito-Lay.

In fact, advertisers spent close to $6 billion dollars in online advertising in 2003, according to Jupiter, and by 2008, they will spend approximately $ 14.8 billion, the same amount spent on magazine advertising. When you consider that magazines have been around since the mid-1700s and the Internet (as a commercial medium) is only about a decade old, that's rather impressive.

The look of online advertising is changing as well. There are two main ways that online advertising is growing – one is through paid search, and the other is through contextual advertising. To get an idea of what paid search is, go to your favorite search engine site (such as Google or Yahoo), type in the word "advertising" and you'll see a list of text-only banners on the top or on the right of your search results. Companies pay for ad space on particular keyword searches. The reason this method of advertising has grown in popularity is because it provides more effective targeting for the advertiser as well as for the consumer. The advertiser spends money to be included only on searches for "advertising," and not on unrelated searches such as "doctors in New York City." The consumer gets access to related resources that he or she might not have found otherwise.

Another new form of online advertising is the contextual ad. Like paid search ads, the contextual ad forges a strong connection between what the consumer is viewing online and the product advertised. Advertisers are taking advantage of the technological capabilities of high-speed broadband Internet connections (cable modem and DSL) to create ads that grab the web user's attention. For example, let's say you are reading *The New York Times* Arts & Leisure section online, and you click on a movie review. All of a sudden you see an online ad for a new film that just opened. What makes this ad different from a simple pop-up ad, which looks like just another open Web window, is that the contextual ad looks like a very short television commercial, using streaming video and audio to display an enticing clip from the new movie. Other advertisers, like Orbitz, actually create mini-games in their advertisements to entice the Web user into spending more time on the ad – and then click through to the site. As online advertisements proliferate, advertisers need targeted, interactive and unusual ads to draw consumers.

Business Climate

Historically, advertising is very sensitive to the state of the economy. If people aren't working, or are afraid of losing their jobs, then they're not buying, and advertising budgets get cut. The result in the recession of 2000-2001 was a dramatic downturn in advertising spending. In 2001, advertising spending as a percentage of GDP experienced the largest single-year drop in history. Since then, the advertising market has followed the general economy in returning to healthier levels of spending. Advertising budgets are still tight, but they are increasing, and agencies are breathing a little easier these days

Robert Coen of Universal McCann, a widely respected and followed forecaster, estimates that the advertising spending in 2004 will grow 6.9 percent from 2003 spending levels. Agencies are once again starting to add staff to accommodate increased spending by their clients. Other, more cautious agencies, are using freelancers full-time.

"It's really crazy sometimes," says a freelance art director for a large promotion agency. "I was working here full-time, was laid-off during the recession, but have been freelancing here and am putting in more hours than when I worked here as a full-time employee! I love it, and I'm making more money doing it." It's definitely a new environment, but marketers and advertising agencies are sufficiently smart, agile and adaptable to operate in it.

Hiring at ad agencies follows significant new business wins, and while there has been a gradual increase in advertising spending since the recession, major new business wins haven't yet translated into an easy job market. However, there are more entry-level openings as the economy starts improving and agencies win some more new business.

Industry Trends

A diversity of choices

The media landscape has changed dramatically since television sets were mass-produced back in the 1950s, and advertisers' choices were limited. There were three television networks, ABC, CBS and NBC; five major magazines, *Time*, *Life*, *Newsweek*, *The Saturday Evening Post* and *Look*, newspapers in every market, and a slew of radio stations programmed primarily for music. Now there are a multitude of media outlets to fit every taste.

Given the diversity of media choices, broadcast television, as differentiated from cable, has been in a continual state of decline. Since 1988, average weekly prime time viewing has dropped precipitously from 10.5 hours per week to less than seven hours per week. Our homes now receive over 63 channels, compared to three in 1950. With print, there are now over four times as many magazine titles to choose from as consumers had in 1950. And in the past few years, other forms of communication have dramatically proliferated as well.

Advertising agencies are continually searching for new media, new forms to expose commercial messages. If imprinting an ad on the backs of turtles reached a wide enough audience and was efficient, you can bet that you would be up to your neck in turtles. Fortunately for turtles, technology is the hottest new media form. "Rapidly emerging technologies will offer new ways to deliver advertising messages and present even more competition for consumers' share of their media time," predicts Eric Ober, former president of *CBS News*. Consider how cell phones have evolved over the last several years – they are now another platform for advertising.

Marketers are finding ways to send product ads to your phone as text messages. Fox's popular television series *American Idol* ran a promotion in April 2003 that encouraged viewers to use their cell phones to participate in on-air polls, enter sweepstakes or to vote for their favorite contestant. The promotion generated 2.5 million responses! Using this SMS ('Short Message System') capability of cell phones does raise important privacy concerns, however, which is why many marketers are being vigilant about securing permission from consumers (usually by asking them to sign up on the web) before sending marketing messages to them.

In the following sections, we'll take a look at some of the more exciting things that are happening in advertising and media technology today.

What's new in TV

Television has lost viewers in almost every demographic group since 2000. No one is exactly sure why, although it probably has to do with many small reasons rather than one big one (e.g., the growth of the Internet, the fact that there are so many more entertainment choices for people today, and that if they wait long enough, people can see their favorite television series on DVD). In any case, network television executives are trying some interesting ideas with their programming schedules to see if they can stanch the flow of viewers, like starting new programs in the summer instead of the fall (when they traditionally have), or creating more short-form programming (short-term event series instead of typical 13-episode series). It remains to be seen whether these methods will have the desired effect, but network television is definitely in for a change.

With Interactive TV (iTV), consumers can buy products and services. The popularity of personal video recorders like TiVo, which allow customers to delete or fast-forward through commercials, is growing. To combat this practice and make their service more attractive to advertisers video-on-demand providers are developing set-top boxes to allow cable and satellite operators to insert one minute of "unskippable" ads every 30 minutes.

With enhanced TV, users can interact with programs and commercials while continuing to watch through picture-in-picture technology. Users click images or icons with their remote controls to request additional information, purchase products and services, respond to polls, games and coupon offers. And synched TV/Web-related content runs in tandem with TV programs. The "dual screen" experience allows viewers to become further engaged in telecasts by interacting with the program in real time. Interactive ads are synched with corresponding TV commercials. For example, a commercial on TV would direct viewers to a web site. The technology requires a TV and a home PC. Advertisers like Mazda, Coca-Cola, AT&T, Kraft and Nabisco have used this technique to generate leads and distribute coupons on programs such as the Oscars and *Monday Night Football*.

What's new in radio

Satellite radio was launched in 2001 and is unique in its ability to offer a consistent signal across the United States with over 120 channels of programming, many of which are unavailable anywhere else. Satellite radio also offers content provided by television networks (CNN, Fox News, The Weather Channel, ABC, and so on). The two big players in this young and emerging market are XM Radio and Sirius, and they have close to 1.5 million subscribers between them. With over 100 channel formats to choose from, satellite radio allows advertisers to narrowly target consumers, albeit less frequently since satellite radio is relatively advertising-free. After a slow start, this medium is gaining momentum among consumers and is growing more quickly than VCRs and cable TV in their early years. Satellite radio is primarily offered as either standard or optional equipment in many new car models, but new versions of the product are available for use in the home.

Internet radio is another recent innovation. This new media takes various forms. One format is music streaming on the computer. Another is traditional radio stations simulcast on the Web. A third includes Internet-only music providers, supplying a wide array of listening choices through streaming music and videos, downloads for MP3 players, music review and a variety of other services. Advertising takes the form of banner or interstitial ads on their web sites and links to retail web sites where the music being played can be purchased. The major advantage of Internet radio is that it offers a way to reach consumers as they spend more time with their computers and less time with traditional media.

Other new media forms

Virtual signage: If you've ever watched football, baseball, golf or the Olympic Games you've seen virtual signage. It's the yellow first down on CBS NFL Football, the location of the hole in golf, the finish line in downhill skiing, and of particular interest to advertisers it's the Coca-Cola logo projected on the fifty-yard line and the AOL logo projected on the dugout wall behind the catcher in baseball. In fact, virtual signage, projected on the side of a building in Midtown Manhattan, is extensively used by CBS News to brand its news programming. Ford, Mastercard, Nordstrom, Harrah's, Shell and Midas utilize this new medium.

Virtual product placement: Virtual product placement, like virtual signage, is the process of placing the advertiser's product within the matrix of a show. A box of Oreo Cookies and a bottle of Pepsi would be projected on a kitchen table, or a tube of Crest on a bathroom shelf. Virtual product placement is currently being tested in television, primarily in syndication. WB Syndication is exploring virtual product placement in reruns of *Friends*, *Will & Grace*, and *The Drew Carey Show*. The cost of placing a product is generally equivalent to the cost of a thirty-second commercial. The advantage of this form is that it provides a "zap-proof" environment. It's impossible to skip the product if it's embedded in a show's content. But the effectiveness of this format looms large. The jury is still out on whether product placement influences purchases.

Blogs (web logs): Web logs are nothing more than online diaries made public – and they are gaining in popularity. According to Perseus Development Corporation, a company that designs software for online surveys, there will be 10 million blogs by the end of 2004. Ninety percent of bloggers are between 13 and 29 years old, and about half of those are between 13 and 19. Blogs are the newest form of online community to pop up, and marketers, ever savvy, are taking advantage of their underground nature to get products noticed by a very fickle crowd. Dr. Pepper/7Up, for example, recently found itself the target of blogging ire when it enlisted six teens to write about Raging Cow flavored milk drinks, one of their new products, in their blogs. When some bloggers found out that "corporate" influence had infiltrated even this grass roots community, they organized a boycott. Whether the boycott or the blogging has any effect remains to be seen, but it certainly got Raging Cow's name on a lot of computer screens! This type of advertising is still uncommon, since the blogging phenomenon has only really reached mainstream notice within the last year or two. Ideas like these can come from the brand team on the client side or the account team on the agency side, and work best when both teams are willing to take a chance on something new and unproven.

Guerilla marketing

A guerilla is a member of a paramilitary unit traveling into enemy territory to conduct surprise raids. That pretty much sums up guerilla marketing. It's unconventional marketing intended to get maximum results from minimal resources, and surprise is an important element. Guerilla marketing typically uses nontraditional media to accomplish its goals of awareness and trial. Large advertisers and small, often to great success, have used the technique.

Guerilla marketing's purpose is to leverage the most persuasive and most elusive form of advertising: word of mouth. Toyota found a way to get the attention of a notoriously difficult market, young men between 18 and 24 years old. In promoting its new Scion beginning in the summer of 2003, it played down the Toyota name and played up the "mystery" factor of the car by parking it outside trendy nightspots and letting club goers 'discover' it on their own. They were curious about the car, told their friends, viral marketing took over and proved the campaign a success.

Overview of Advertising Agencies

CHAPTER 2

There are three basic types of advertising agencies – full service agencies, creative boutiques, and media planning and buying agencies.

Full-Service Agencies

Full-service agencies are typically large companies with offices and clients throughout the United States and the world. Clients might range from illustrious household names like Ford, IBM and American Express (who may commit to ad campaigns costing tens or hundreds of millions of dollars) to less well-known companies spending under a million dollars.

As befits their name, full-service agencies provide their clients with a full range of services. These include:

- **Marketing strategy development** – This department creates a strategy to build and sell a brand to the most receptive audience.
- **Ad creation** – Home to a bevy of creative types – art directors who design the advertising, and copywriters who craft words into a selling proposition.
- **Media planning** – This departemnt conducts research to find the proper demographics for an advertising campaign.
- **Media buying** – The process of purchasing selected media based on appropriate demographics for an advertising campaign.
- **Account planning/research** – Devoted to determining the quantitative and qualitative factors affecting consumer perception and attitudes. For example, a certain car is seem as "feminine," decreasing its appeal to a male audience.
- **Production** – The process of physically transforming an advertising strategy into a print or broadcast advertisement.

Up to the early 1970s, advertising agencies prided themselves on providing other services, like sales promotion, direct response and public relations, all in the same company. Ad professionals were typically generalists, creating advertising, direct response and sales promotion as part of one package deal. The mid-1970s marked a sea change in the agency landscape. Agencies began to realize that these services, which they had given away for free could become profit-generating businesses of their own and spun them off. (In some cases, these spin-offs remained under the company umbrella, so there might be XYZ Advertising, XYZ Public Relations and XYZ Direct Response.)

Today's full-service advertising agencies concentrate only on advertising. If clients want direct response, public relations or other non-advertising services, they must buy them separately. Clients sometimes pick and choose, contracting with one agency for creative work, another for media planning and a third for direct response mailing, or they may purchase all services from a single agency.

Large full-service agencies offer employees a great deal of opportunity for movement within the company, both between departmens and around the globe. "After a successful career in the New York office of Ogilvy & Mather, I was transferred to London to run a major client," says Tim Sickinger, formerly a senior vice president of Ogilvy & Mather. "For a guy from Omaha, it was a terrific experience."

Among the top full-service agencies are Young & Rubicam (known as Y&R Advertising), Ogilvy & Mather Worldwide, BBDO Worldwide, McCannErickson Worldwide, DDB Worldwide, J. Walter Thompson Co., Leo Burnett Co., FCB Worldwide and Saatchi & Saatchi. These agencies are the giants of the industry.

Over the past decade, there has been quite a bit of consolidation in the ad industry. Most major ad agencies are now owned by six major holding companies. These holding companies (ranked in order of total size) are:

1. Omnicom Group (owns BBDO Worldwide and DDB Worldwide)
2. Interpublic Group of Companies (owns FCB Worldwide and McCann-Erickson Worldwide)
3. WPP Group (owns J. Walter Thompson Co., Ogilvy & Mather Worldwide and Y&R Advertising)
4. Publicis Groupe (owns Leo Burnett Co. and Saatchi & Saatchi)
5. Dentsu (the largest ad firm in Japan)
6. Havas (owns Arnold Worldwide and Euro RSCG Tatham Partners)

Source: Advertising Age, 2003

Creative Boutiques

In addition to these full-service agencies, there are also creative boutiques providing a narrower range of services – and a rather noncorporate company culture.

The only service creative boutiques offer is the inception and production of advertising. Typically, the founders are "creatives," copywriters and/or art directors with established reputations who have decided to leave the full service agency environment. Boutiques tend to be independently owned, relatively small in size and focused on developing effective, creative campaigns. Clients, large and small, use creative-only agencies for a variety of reasons:

- To explore alternate creative approaches to existing campaigns
- To rejuvenate tired brands with fresh creative thinking
- To save money on creative
- To keep current agencies on their toes

Because of the focus on creative work, creative boutiques can be stimulating and enjoyable, not to mention kooky, places to work. But because of their size, job opportunities can be more difficult to find. Two of the more well-known boutique agencies are Mad Dogs and Englishmen in San Francisco and New York and Cliff Freeman and Partners in New York. (Cliff Freeman and Partners created Staples' long-running "Yeah, we got that" campaign.) A quick way to understand the difference between the large full-service agencies and the smaller, creatively oriented agencies is to visit their web sites (maddogsandenglishmen.com and clifffreemanandpartners.com) – you'll see they have a distinct sense of humor. Mad Dogs & Englishmen, for example, has a webcam set up so you can see what's happening in their offices 24/7!

Media Agencies

As opposed to creative agencies, which offer only creative services, media agencies offer only media planning and buying services. Their pitch is that they plan and buy media more efficiently and effectively than media departments of full service agencies. Among the top media agencies are Starcom MediaVest, MindShare, OMD and Initiative Media.

Specialized Agencies

Health care

Some markets are so specialized that they call for advertisers who are well-versed in the intricacies and jargon of the field. That's why there are advertising boutiques that specialize in health care advertising. While these agencies are structured just like other agencies, the target for their advertising is much more specialized. These agencies must be able to appeal to, brand to and sell to doctors, nurses and health care administrators.

Some leading health care agencies are KPR, CommonHealth, Euro RSCGLife Becker, Grey Healthcare Group, FCB HealthCare and Medicus Group International.

Ethnic advertising agencies

Increasingly, marketers are turning to ethnic advertising agencies to better target ethnic and other minorities, including blacks, Hispanics, Asians and gays. Just as health care advertising agencies must be immersed in the language of doctors and administrators, ethnic advertisers are sensitive and familiar with the cultures and messages inherent in minority cultures.

The following are the top ethnic advertising agencies.

- **African American** – Burrell Communications Group, Uniworld Group, Carol H. Williams Advertising
- **Hispanic** – Bravo Group, Bromley Communications, Zubi Creative Strategies
- **Asian** – A Partnership, Kang & Lee, Mosaica

Direct response agencies

Direct response agencies create campaigns that ask consumers to directly respond to the advertiser by mail, telephone, e-mail, or some other means of communication. Every time you see a TV commercial asking you to respond to an 800 number, or receive a mailing stuffed with offers, or a telemarketer's phone call, you have experienced the handiwork of direct response agencies. These are structured just like full service advertising agencies and offer the same services. The top direct response agencies are, Draft Worldwide, Rapp

Collins Worldwide, Digitas, TMP Worldwide, Ogilvy One Worldwide, and Grey Direct.

Sales promotion agencies

Promotion agencies primarily use incentives – contests, sweepstakes, coupons, refunds and games to involve consumers in the brand experience. The top promotion agencies are DVC Worldwide, Carlson Marketing Group, Brand Buzz, Momentum and Don Jagoda Associates.

Public Relations Agencies

Public relations firms communicate with various sectors of the public to influence attitudes and opinions in the interest of promoting a person, product or idea. While advertising agencies construct ads and place them in the appropriate media, public relations agencies attempt to influence the media to write or televise their client. Among the top companies are, Hill & Knowlton, Burson-Marsteller, Edelman and Manning, Selvage & Lee. While public relations is often conflated with advertising, as they are both involved in building brands for clients, the methods are rather different.

In-House Agencies

Some companies choose to keep their advertising in-house, though in-house represents a small percentage of the advertising industry. In small firms, the owner or CEO might assume all advertising, promotions, marketing, sales, and public relations responsibilities. But at larger firms, advertising is almost never created by in-house personnel, though some do have strategic advertising capabilities. One recent example is Gateway, which established an in-house agency in 2002. The in-house managers develop the firm's strategies, identify potential markets, pricing strategies, monitor trends, develop new products and services and keep close tabs on the competition. Creative and production work, however, is still outsourced to private agencies.

ON THE JOB

The Jobs

CHAPTER 3

Organizationally, advertising agencies are divided into seven major departments, as shown below.

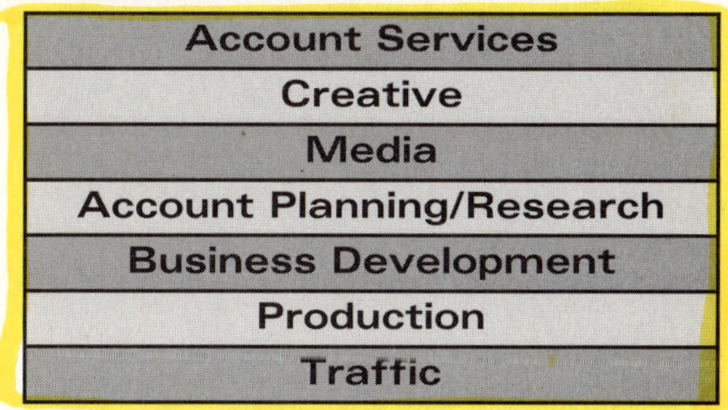

In terms of skills, with the exception of creative, which requires a demonstrated talent for writing or designing ads, a broad-based education, intellectual curiosity, and a love of advertising is all that's essential for most advertising jobs.

In this chapter we'll provide an inside glimpse at these major departments, with special in-depth looks at the three largest departments (account services, creative services and media services). Please note that the provided salary data is for large and medium-sized agencies ($50 million or more in billings).

Account Services

Account services professionals manage the relationship between the agency and the client. They are the first line of contact with the client – and the first line of defense. Essentially, they are the project managers for advertising client accounts.

The account services hierarchy ranges from account coordinator at the entry level, to account directors (also called management supervisors) who oversee one or more client relationships in their entirety. Account services people are marketing and communications consultants; they must know as much about the brand as the client, and more about how to advertise it.

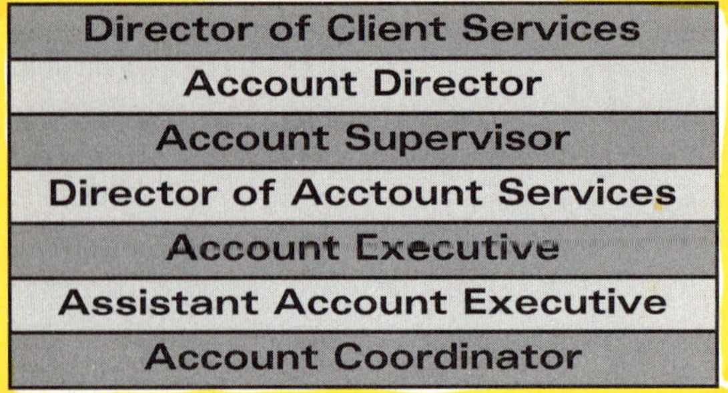

Professional characteristics

Successful account services pros must be all of the following.

- **Integrators.** Account people craft the communications marketing plan and insure that all of the agency's resources are working together to make the plan a reality.
- **Organized.** Account services professionals are detail-oriented, and masters of multi-tasking and following up. They are keepers of the overall timetable for ad production, placement and communication.
- **Generalists.** They must have a working knowledge of every agency discipline ranging from evaluating copy and art to media and production.
- **Advocates.** They are the client's advocate within the agency, and the agency's advocate to the client. Diplomacy and eloquence are key.
- **Students and lovers of advertising.** They must immerse themselves in advertising and marketing and learn the lessons of past and current successes and failures.
- **Cheerleaders.** As leaders of the team, account people must be superb "people" people, exhibiting grace under pressure. "When everyone's walking around moping because the client hates the new campaign, or there's been a screw up somewhere, it's my job to get everyone back on track. In account services, the glass is always half full," an account supervisor at a large agency notes (cheerfully).

One downside of account services: it can be a thankless job to try to get results from people who don't report to you but from whom you need important information, often very quickly. For example, let's say you are an assistant account executive and your manager, the account executive, has a client meeting. Your manager would like to show the client the latest media plan and creative revisions for a specific brand. She asks you to get them for her. You run to the media department and ask for the latest media plan. They tell you that creative hasn't given them the final specs for the ad (is it a half-page magazine ad or a full-page ad?) That affects the media plan, because it might be more efficient to run a half-page ad in some publications but a full-page ad in others. So you run over to creative. They have mocked up both ad sizes but don't know which the client will prefer, so they've left a message for the account executive! You need cooperation and results from several different departments in order to get your own job done, and sometimes that's tough to get.

> "I can't imagine being in this business unless you love it," says an account executive at a small New York agency. "But in order to understand the business you have to know about its history, the old classic campaigns and why they were classics. Campaigns work for a reason."

Salaries and hours

Depending on the size of the agency, its geographic location, and a professional's experience level, salaries will range from $25,000 per year for an account coordinator, up several hundred thousand dollars per year for a management supervisor. Although client accounts may be seasonal, the agency business is not. Depending on the account you're assigned to, the workweek can range from 40 to 60 hours. Typical salaries are as follows: director of client services ($300K+), account director ($100K-$300K), account supervisor ($75K-$100K), account executive ($45K-$60K), assistant account executive ($25K-$35K), and account coordinator ($20K-$25K).

Media Services

Broadly, media services is responsible for the planning and buying of print, broadcast, out-of-home (billboards) and interactive media in the most effective and efficient way possible. Media planners are the strategists – they determine when and where it's most advantageous to buy advertising space for any given campaign. Buyers actually negotiate for, and purchase, the media space.

But that's hardly the whole story. These media specialists are also key members of the advertising branding team. They must find environments that extend and reinforce the brand image of their clients – and buy space for advertising those brands. Armed with consumer research, both proprietary and purchased, media professionals not only know the target audience's media habits the programs they watch and listen to, the magazines and newspapers they read – they also know what influences consumers to make purchasing decisions. Purchase decision influencers are people who have a lot of influence over the purchase but aren't the "target market." For example, while men may purchase suits, women have significant influence over which suits their male partners and companions buy.

The result of their research and work is the media plan for the advertising campaign. Major media outlets will then compete to get on the plan (that is, to secure a portion of the client's ad budget for their magazine or television network or newspaper). The plan itself contains recommendations on where the client should spend their media budget to achieve the campaign's goals in the most efficient way. The plan outlines how many people the media recommendation reaches, how many times the commercial or print ad will run, and the total audience impressions the plan will attract.

Once the plan is approved, media vehicles like television stations, newspapers and magazines that weren't included in the plan fight to get included. So, in the midst of a buy, buyers not only have to contend with the job of purchasing media, they also have to entertain presentations from disappointed media sales reps. Media buyers, especially, frequently socialize with sales representatives from media organizations on a regular basis.

Executive Media Director
Media Director
Associate Media Director
Supervisor
Buyer/Planner
Assistant Buyer/Planner

Professional characteristics

Media people are:

- **Analytical and detail oriented.** Media is very much about numbers, but numbers are not the whole story. Media planners must use syndicated research and judgment to select media that delivers the appropriate demographics and psychographics. But being a good media planner also requires common sense. Planners and buyers are given budgets of millions, even hundreds of millions of dollars. It's their job to analyze the numbers – ratings, share, circulation – of potential media buys, and then look beyond the numbers. A commercial for denture adhesives aimed at an older target audience, wouldn't make sense on *Friends*, even though *Friends* may deliver a fairly large older audience.

- **Salespeople.** Every recommendation, every plan, must be sold internally and to the client. And you need to be attuned to what the client really wants. Sometimes the client wants to run his ad in his favorite magazine, logic be damned. But let's say that, based on the quantitative analysis the media planners have done (Are the magazine demographics appropriate for the client's product? Is the price to advertise in the magazine reasonable, or is it expensive? If you advertise in this magazine, do you have to cut another that might be more appropriate for the product?), it's been determined that this particular magazine doesn't really belong on the plan. So you need to be a skilled salesperson to convince the client that their favorite magazine just won't work.

- **Organized.** When you control the expenditure of millions of dollars of someone else's money, you had better be organized and able to account for every dollar.

- **Good negotiators,** This talent is especially important for media buyers. Buyers regard rate card prices – the official cost of a media unit – as just the first step of negotiation. Media is a true supply and demand marketplace and prices continually fluctuate.

Salaries and hours

Salaries range from $20,000 per year for an assistant to several hundred thousand dollars a year for a media director. The salaries: executive vice presedent and media director ($300K+), media director ($250K), associate media director ($125K-$150K), supervisor ($80K-$90K), buyers/planners ($60K-$80K), assistants ($25K-$30K).

A typical workweek of 50 hours is not uncommon, and can reach 60-70+ when timing is factored in (hours lengthen just before a media plan is due) along with the social events that occur after working hours. Granted, those events can be enjoyable (tickets to sporting events, dinner and the theater with the advertising sales reps), but they make for a long workweek nonetheless.

Creative Services

Many people outside of the industry view creative as the "romance" part of the business. Romantic and exciting though it may seem, copywriting and art direction is hard work. Creative services jobs are indeed exciting, but failure is easy to come by.

Once the creative strategy is set (by the account services folks) and approved by the client, and once the consumer research has been transformed into a media plan, it's time for the Big Idea – a creative translation of the strategy into a compelling and persuasive ad. And there is nothing more difficult than facing a hard deadline and sitting at a desk, well into the night, staring at a blank sheet of paper, in an office littered with balled up sheets of paper, while thinking, "Lord, send me an idea!"

Copywriters, who write the copy (words, script, whatever) and art directors, who visually design the ads, work as a team. Together, they create ads, not only for the current campaigns but for "back up" – campaigns that are continually tested in the event that the current advertising loses its effectiveness, or "wears out" – campaigns as well.

The creative process, for new ads, is initiated by the client. Let's say the client calls the account executive and requests a four-color ad for *Modern Maturity* magazine. The account executive writes a creative strategy statement for the ad (obviously aimed at an older audience) and takes it to the creative supervisor. The creative supervisor assigns the ad to a copywriter and art director team with a due date. Once the ad is completed and approved internally, the copy and layout are presented to the client.

Creative Director	
Copy Head	Art Head
Supervisor	Supervisor
Copywriter	Art Director

Professional characteristics

Copywriters and art directors must:

- **Have dancing minds.** The creative process is often a journey of serendipity – making fortunate discoveries by accident. The creative mind allows these discoveries or insights to happen on a subconscious level and then consciously acts on them. "You never know where or when an idea comes," said an art director at a large agency. "I could be watching a movie, and all of a sudden something clicks, and all I want to do is rush back to the office to get it down on paper."

- **Be students of advertising.** Good creatives are aware of what's current and what has come before. The secrets of advertising are contained in the history of the great ads. Some notable campaigns are Apple Computer's "1984" commercial that introduced the Macintosh computer; the Wendy's "Where's the Beef?" campaign, and the Ad Council's Smokey the Bear Forest Fire Prevention campaign, which began in 1944 and is still running today!

- **Be aware of what your colleagues are doing.** Smart creatives know who is doing great work, who isn't, and why it matters – after all, some of them are producing ads for your client's competition! A bible of the field is *Communication Arts*, a design magazine known for discovering and acknowledging fresh ideas in print and advertising. (Check out the web site at www.commarts.com.)

- **Be students of human behavior.** Creatives are sensitive to the world they live in. They have to know what's hot and what's not, what's on the edge and what's overplayed. Smart copywriters and art directors immerse themselves in the latest trends, whether it's fashion, cinema, literature or politics.

- **Be good salespeople.** Often, several copywriter and art director teams are designated to work on a campaign. Although the creative strategy sets the boundaries of the creative effort, there's still a lot of room to be different and effective. Smart creative people know how to sell to the agency and the client.

- **Be skilled in the basics of their craft.** Copywriters are masters of language and grammar, and art directors are masters of the visual arts. A 30-second commercial costs hundred of thousands of dollars to produce, and hundreds of thousands more to place in a television show. At those prices each ad is precious. The actors must be properly cast, the lines delivered without a hitch and the setting and wardrobe believable.

- **Be resilient.** Rejection comes with the territory. Before an ad ever gets to the client it's examined internally. Some ads make the grade, many do not.

- **Be disciplined.** Ad making doesn't happen in a vacuum. Every ad must meet the objective standard of the creative strategy statement. Is the promise clear and convincing? Is there sufficient support for the promise? Is the tone appropriate? Is it single-minded?

- **Be businesspeople.** It won't do to create an ad that costs $100,000 when the budget is $25,000.

- **Art directors** must have had some training in film, layout, photography and typography, and above all, good taste.

The Internal Battle for Recognition

"Sometimes, especially in new business presentations, it's like *Mad Max, Beyond Thunderdome*, you know where they put guys in a cage, and the last man standing wins," says a copy supervisor. "You're competing against the other guys, and they're your friends, and it gets wild. I remember once, we were working on an airline pitch and my boss, the creative director, spent fifty thousand dollars on the campaign he created! He commissioned original music, went out and filmed his commercials, and did just about everything he could to sink everybody else's work. He didn't even want to show my campaign to the account group. Hell, I was a junior writer, but I thought my campaign was better. I showed it to an account supervisor who agreed. Not only did my work get presented, it ultimately won the business. The creative director wasn't happy, but what could he do?"

Salaries and hours

Given the peculiar unpredictability of the creative process, the workweek may be long, up to 60 hours per week, but there is some freedom vis a vis the time one arrives for work. Salaries will range from $30,000 per year for junior art directors and copywriters, to $180,000-$200,000 for supervisors, and $400,000-$500,000 for the creative director.

Account Planning, Business Development, Traffic and Production

While account services, media services and creative services are the major avenues for entering the advertising industry, there are other ad career specialties that are worth a look.

Account planning/research

Account planning, an import from British advertising agencies, is a relatively new discipline in the United States. Most of the larger agencies and many of the smaller ones have embraced it. Account planning uses qualitative research to determine why consumers behave the way they do. Planners function as the voice of the consumer within the agency, and their main goal is to gain a deeper understanding of the way consumers react to their clients' product or service. Planners burrow into the consumer's mind, plumbing for insights about the product, its position and competition, and research is their tool. They live with the brand and its consumers. The insights they gain are considered the target market's psychographics – their attitudes, opinions and values. These consumer psychographics help copywriters and art directors create more effective advertising.

To obtain their insights, account planners visit with customers, conduct focus groups and telephone interviews and observe current and potential customers interacting with the clients' product or service. "Interviewing is an art form in search of a deeper truth," said Pen Pendleton, senior vice president for account planning at Rubin Postaer and Associates. "The most brilliantly conceived marketing plan is nothing if the copywriter or art director can't make an ad. Account planners generally work alone and are as curious as hell. You have to be to uncover the gold nuggets that are buried in consumers' minds." Typically about 40 percent of an account planner's time is spent on new business pitches, since demonstrating a firm understanding of the potential client's target market is a critical step in gaining credibility and, hopefully, the business. A love of ads, determination, curiosity and a continuing desire to challenge conventional wisdom are the requisites for the job.

The flip side of account planning is quantitative research. In the larger agencies, the functions of account planning and quantitative research are divided. In many agencies, however, account planning incorporates both qualitative and quantitative research. The goal of quantitative research is to determine the "facts" of consumers and their behavior. Using sophisticated techniques, researchers determine demographics (such things as age, gender, occupation, education), purchase and usage patterns, brand and advertising awareness and other issues that are crucial to understanding the consumer and making ads. Strong analytical skills are a plus for a researcher. Successful account planners and researchers possess not only a love of advertising, but also inquisitiveness and a somewhat "cynical" eye towards what they see. Put more simply, they aren't so quick to take what they see at face value – their curiosity about human nature motivates them to look deeper. Researchers and planners are able to step outside of their own skin to get a better understanding of the clients' target market, and understand how advertising can really work to influence their attitudes and behavior.

Depending on experience, salaries range from $30,000-$35,000 for entry-level jobs to $160,000 for a department head. The workweek can reach 60 hours a week, depending on client deadlines.

Business development

Business development professionals concentrate on getting new business for the ad agency. The department is usually small but the work is intense. Every agency has a "wish list" of clients it would like to work for, or categories (airlines, pharmaceutical, financial services, etc.) it wants to target. It's business development's job to make that happen. Ogilvy & Mather, for example, keeps a roster of clients it would like to work for and regularly contacts them with agency material. For example, the agency produced a series of ads promoting its expertise in certain areas, e.g. "What Ogilvy Has Learned About Financial Advertising," or packaged goods, or automotive, or what have you. Every agency has its unique technique of business development, though the objective is always to ensure a place on a client's short list when it is ready to consider new agencies. Business development departments are usually small. Entry-level salaries start at about $25,000 per year and range up to several hundred thousand dollars for the head of the department.

Traffic

Traffic managers are the keepers of the creative process – schedules and approvals reside in their domain. If account services professionals are like the generals, setting and managing the overall strategy, traffickers are the foot soldiers and work with creative, media and the account group to insure that all deadlines are met. Print publications and broadcast stations have unchangeable closing dates. In addition, it's traffic's responsibility to see that the ads are approved at every stage of their development and forwarded to the media on time. Successful traffic managers are organized, detail-oriented and able to work under pressure. It is a difficult, highly stressful job. The benefit is that you get to interact with virtually every department in the agency, and you get a bird's eye view of what their jobs are really like. Salaries range from $25,000 at entry level, $50,000 per year at supervisory levels and $100,000 for the department head. The workweek can easily top 50 hours.

Production

There are two types of production specialists at advertising agencies – print and broadcast. Print production specialists are schooled in every aspect of the print production process and are experts at making ads look great in magazines, newspapers and out-of-home venues. Most print production advertising professionals are hired from printing companies and other graphic design outlets.

Broadcast producers are in charge of the actual production of TV and radio commercials. They work closely with the creative department to select directors, production facilities, talent, music and just about every other aspect of broadcast production. Like their sisters and brothers in print production, broadcast producers are well-organized, able to work well under pressure, and experts at their craft.

The workweek for both print and broadcast production can stretch up to 50 hours. Print production salaries range from $25,000 to $75,000 per year. Broadcast producers earn the same starting salary, though top players routinely earn in excess of $150,000.

A Word On Moving Between Departments

Assume you're hired as a traffic manager. Does that mean that you're destined to be in traffic until you retire? Not at all. Assistants often become account people, creatives move into account services, media people move into account planning. The path isn't easy, but it happens all the time. Generally, there is no agency policy prohibiting interdepartmental movement. "It's really up to the supervisor," says an associate media director. "Some supervisors believe that if you're in media, you made your choice and that's that. To change, you have to leave the agency. But life is long, and supervisors come and go. I began my career in media, and after a couple of years I decided to switch to account work. My supervisor didn't have a problem. I made the switch and after a few months I realized that I hated it. I guess I didn't like being in the line of fire every minute of every day. I wanted out, and media welcomed me back with open arms."

Once you're working in an agency, especially if it's your first job, it's going to take a while to get a sense of what's going on. You may decide that you love what you do. Great! But if you don't, there's still hope. "I started in account services," says a former creative director. "It was fine, and I enjoyed it. But I also loved to travel and started writing about it. First, columns in my local paper and then travel books. I found that I really liked to write. I approached the creative director and he saw my work and offered me a job as a junior writer on a hotel account, at a lot less money. I took the risk, and it ultimately paid off."

Making friends in other departments helps facilitate internal movement. Jennifer, an account executive, started as an administrative assistant at a small agency and developed a good working relationship with her boss. When her boss left to take a higher-level position at a larger agency, her boss hired Jennifer as an assistant account executive, and Jennifer has never looked back. Doors are always open in ad agencies. Walk in and introduce yourself. Ask people about their jobs.

Look Before You Leap

Do you still think a career in advertising is right for you? Consider these facts before making the leap.

1. **Advertising is a service business.** The dictionary defines "service" as the "occupation or duties of a servant." Many advertising people bristle at the notion of their profession as a form of servitude. They much prefer the term "marketing partner" to describe the relationship between advertiser and client. It implies a utopian equality that is something to strive for but really doesn't exist. From the chairman to the mailroom sorters, advertising agency employees serve the interests of their clients, the interests of their agency and the interests of their stockholders (if public). "The client puts food on my table and clothes on my back. If it wasn't for the client I wouldn't have a job," says an account director. "And everyone who works for me better understand that." At the end of the day it's the client's money, and money equals control.

2. **Advertising agencies are pressure cookers.** Deadlines are the bane of the business. Every work product in every department is subject to deadlines. "Client needs it first thing in the morning!" insists the account executive, or "The art and mechanicals have to go to the printer tonight!" yells the traffic manager. Media calls, "Unless you want to run 'Compliments of a Friend' instead of the new four color spread, you had better get that ad released to *Sports Illustrated* now!" Even with the best intentions and the best planning, things inevitably go wrong and tempers flare. "Things can get pretty hot around here sometimes," says a copywriter. "Ads are due, and people are running in and out of your office asking where they are, and there's nothing you can do about it. It's the nature of the beast!"

3. **There's no place to hide.** Advertising is not for the faint of heart. Every person on the account is visible, warts and all, to the client and other members of the agency team. Everyone has to pull his or her weight. An advertising agency is very much like a small town, and an account is roughly equivalent to a family. Word travels fast, good and bad. The stars, the achievers and the poor performers are quickly identified. "At one agency I worked at, there was a separate dining room for senior vice presidents and above," says one experienced ad professional. "It was a very nice place with china and tablecloths. Every now and again, someone at the table would mention the name of an employee he was considering hiring into his group. Usually, most people would have positive comments. But on the rare occasion, the

comment would be 'Jim Smith? Yeah, I worked with him. I guess he's all right. It was the kiss of death, and Jim's career would be over, at this agency at least. He never knew where the arrow came from."

It is not uncommon for clients to ask that an individual be removed from their account or insist that certain individuals be retained or promoted on their businesses. To insure the quality of its staff, agencies perform rigorous, regular evaluations to grade staff. That grade determines raises, bonuses and in some cases, continued employment.

4. **Advertising is a team sport.** The word "team" is used so often today that it's become almost meaningless. But not in advertising. Accounts couldn't operate without smoothly functioning, hardworking teams. Teamwork is fostered in a variety of ways. Some agencies maintain softball teams and participate in inter-agency leagues, others have outings, an afternoon or an evening away from work. Still others offer cash bonuses to award winning campaigns. "Ogilvy had all sorts of activities for its employees to participate in," says Robin Abrutyn, formerly of Ogilvy & Mather's media department. "It helped me get to know other people at the agency, and make friends." Whatever the technique, the goal is to strengthen the bonds that tie the teams together. Advertising agencies are not friendly places for slackers. Everyone is accountable.

5. **Job security can be iffy.** Account movement is an industry fact of life and the average life of an agency account is roughly four years. Clients move their accounts for a variety of reasons – the creative product has gone stale, key agency staff members have left, sales are slipping, new client management has a relationship with other agencies – but whatever the reason, the human toll can be great. "I've been through one agency-wide layoff and it wasn't pretty," says an account executive. "After 15 years with the agency, the client called for a review and invited other agencies to pitch for its business. We made the finals, but that's it. Fifty people were laid off. It took four months to get another job." Although agencies often do their best to retain staff after an account loss, especially if they're good, it only works if there's new business to replace lost business.

6. **Your life is often not your own.** See point number one. If you're expecting to work nine to five, you're in for a shock. People are usually at their desks between 8 and 8:30 in the morning – earlier if an early morning meeting is scheduled, and you're part of it (or responsible for setting up the conference room). The business day ends when it ends. Ten-hour days are common and weekends are often used to catch up.

When you're sitting in meetings all day the work piles up. Agencies are rife with stories about cancelled dates, missed birthdays, anniversaries, graduations and just about anything else you might plan, including vacations. "I missed too many important events in my family's life," says a management supervisor. "Luckily, I have an understanding husband, and kids who accept the career that I've chosen. What helps to make up for it is the high that I get from the work."

7. **Only "people people" need apply**. Becoming a skilled advertising practitioner isn't as hard as, say, astrophysics. You learn the rules and apply them. But there's another side to the equation, and that's learning the fine art of persuasion. The agency is filled with people who don't report to you, yet they're essential to your job. Some are cranky, some live in a fantasy land, some are difficult, some treat schedules with disdain and some will make you totally crazy.

Assume for a moment that you're an account executive. At best, you'll have an assistant as a direct report. How do you get everyone else – media, creative, production, research, your bosses and clients – to share your vision? "In a way, life in an agency is a popularity contest. First, they better like you," says an account director at a Los Angeles agency. "And that only happens when you support, encourage, demonstrate a clear appreciation of their problems and stick your neck out for them. Do all of that and you've got them. Saying "thank you," and meaning it, every chance you get, is a good first step."

Creating A Campaign

CHAPTER 4

A campaign is a series of ads on television, radio, the Internet, magazines, out-of home and newspapers that reinforce the brand image and promise. Here's how a brand ad campaign for an imaginary credit card might work.

The game is afoot

Let's call our brand the Premium Gold Credit Card. Premium Gold has been around for years but it's a "me, too" product, just another piece of plastic in the wallet. For some reason Premium Gold hasn't successfully differentiated itself from its competition. Its customer base is not growing. Premium Gold's chief marketing officer decides it's time for a change and announces an agency review for her $50 million account. She sends out requests for proposal (RFP) and a questionnaire to 20 agencies with credit card/financial services experience and reputations for outstanding creative work. The RFP is the first round in the process.

After reviewing the RFPs she narrows the list down and invites six advertising agencies to pitch for the business. The chief marketing officer presents the problem – Premium Gold is not growing and is indistinguishable from its competitors – and asks for solutions. The only agency in the finals without credit card or financial services experience is AMA Partners, a hot, full-service agency known for breakthrough creative work and marketing smarts. AMA has wanted a credit card account for years and has been in several competitions for other, larger card accounts, but has never made the final cut.

Building the Team

The first thing that AMA does is assign a team of 15 people to work on the new business presentation, which is three months away. The size of the team varies with the importance of the prospective client's business, and Premium Gold is important to AMA. Every team member will have to do double duty and work nights and weekends, since they must continue to work on their own accounts, which doesn't seem to matter. "New business is the lifeblood of an agency, generating jobs, bonuses and opportunity," says Chuck Bachrach of Rubin Postaer Associates. "It's really hard work, but it's what the business is all about." Excitement is in the air, even though AMA has only one chance in six of winning.

The group includes account services professionals (ranging from management supervisors to account coordinators) whose job it is to coordinate and lead the presentation, and to develop the positioning, creative and marketing strategies and the advertising plan. Copywriters will write the ad content, and art directors will design the ads. Account planners will be responsible for qualitative research, getting out and talking to people to search for insights into consumer attitudes about Premium Gold. Media researchers will analyze existing quantitative research to determine the audience. Media planners will determine the appropriate media forms and frequency, as well as the budgets necessary to reach the target audience. Print and broadcast production people will produce sample ads and storyboard TV commercials. And finally, a representative from traffic and production will make sure that everything comes together in time for the presentation.

Because AMA is a firm believer in integrated marketing (building brands using a variety of marketing techniques) representatives from AMA's sales promotion, direct response and public relations subsidiary agencies are also part of the team and will support AMA's brand building efforts. Advertising's job is to reposition the company and communicate the new positioning through mass media. Through database marketing, direct response's job is to create programs that find new, and strengthen existing, relationships with loyal customers. Sales promotion will create incentive programs that generate immediate awareness, trial or repurchase using sweepstakes, contests, games and coupons. Public relations will create events and other activities designed to ensure Premium Gold's positive public image by helping people understand its products and services. All the elements in the marketing mix will be integrated to ensure that Premium Gold's new brand image will be consistent in look, feel and tone in every customer message.

Account Services

Because account services is running this effort, the management supervisor and the account supervisor receive carloads of material containing all of Premium Gold's past and current consumer research, copies of its marketing and media plans, and copies of previous and current advertising campaigns. Account services disseminates this material to the appropriate AMA groups working on the presentation. The department also sets a timetable of "drop dead" decision and work completion dates for all of the agency groups. To keep things simple, if additional information is needed, account services is the only group permitted to contact the client.

The first order of business is to find out everything there is to know about Premium Gold's customers. Who are they? Why do they use the card? If they don't use it, why not? How do they use the card? How old are they? Where do they live? How much do they earn? What are their attitudes toward the card, positive or negative? What benefits would they like to see added or dropped? And, most vital, did Premium Gold's previous agency miss anything important?

First, the account planners get to work. They hold focus groups (small groups of consumers) with whom they meet to discuss Premium Gold, determining how the card is perceived and used, and looking for emotional connections a campaign can build upon. In fact, one account planner has been deputized to live with a Premium Gold cardholder family for a week to see what he can learn. After this data has been collected and analyzed, the branding begins. Account planning has uncovered some very important information. Premium Gold's customer base skews young (men and women 18-34) and senior (men and women 50+). They also discover that the card is used disproportionately for travel-related expenses.

With the new definition of the customer in hand, account services creates a positioning statement – a simple statement of how a brand is perceived in the minds of the target market. This positioning statement is then vetted with those focus groups. Once the positioning is set, account services professionals can create an overall marketing strategy to brand Premium Gold. Within it are sub-strategies for every tool in an agency's arsenal: copy, media, sales promotion, public relations and direct response. Think of the marketing strategy as a pie in which advertising is one huge slice.

The winning positioning statement is "The credit card designed especially for people who travel." Based on this statement, account services writes the creative strategy. Only when they are finished will the creatives – the copywriters and the ad directors – construct ads for various media that fall within the bounds of this strategic plan.

The positioning statement

A positioning statement formally stakes out where you are placing the brand among its competition and what unique selling proposition you are assigning to it. It's the strategy of the campaign, what you refer to in order to make sure you are staying on course. Creative can get pretty wild and off track, so you always go back to the positioning statement to say, "Does this support what we are saying about the brand?"

> **"Give me the freedom of a tight creative strategy statement,"**
> *– Piet Verbeck, formerly Creative Director of Ogilvy Partners*

There are five essential elements in the Premium Gold creative strategy statement.

- **Objective** – Convince the target audiences that Premium Gold is the preferred travel card.
- **Target Audience** – Men and women 18-34 and 50+ who live in urban areas with household incomes of $75,000+
- **Key Benefit/Promise** – Premium Gold is the preferred travel card
- **Support** – Concierge service, discounts on hotels, car rentals, airlines, restaurants, theme parks, discounts at Outward Bound, and travel planning advice.
- **Tone and manner** – Fun. On the go.

The Creative Team

The creatives must now create a brand and stake a claim to a bit of real estate in the consumers' mind and heart. Repetition is the soul of advertising simply because memories are short. Most people can barely remember what they had for dinner last night, much less an ad that glances past their minds like a stone skipping over water. Sameness defines a campaign; the same message over and over again, well told, until it worms its way into the consumer's consciousness. Boring? To some, perhaps. Effective advertising? Absolutely. In advertising, this "sameness" is usually expressed in four ways:

1. Look. This is the art director's job. Each ad in the campaign must look like the ones that came before it, in broadcast and in print. A good test is to tack the ads to a wall. The headlines and visuals will be different, of course, but the ads should appear to belong to the same family. Is the typeface consistent? Is the layout unique? Consider the U.S. Army advertising campaign, "An Army of One." Each of the commercials and print ads features a different ruggedly handsome (or tomboyishly lovely) American fighting machine. It almost doesn't matter what the body copy says; viewers get the idea. They know instantly that it's a U.S. Army commercial.

2. Words. This is the copywriter's job. A unique set of words brands the product or service and distinguishes it from competition. American Express wrapped an implicit promise in a warning: "The American Express Card. Don't Leave Home Without It." Coca-Cola promised, "The Pause That Refreshes." And Maxwell House Coffee offers a consistently good taste experience with, "Good To the Last Drop."

3. A unique sound. This is specially important for radio. The sound can be a voice (Frosted Flake's Tony the Tiger or the Green Giant's "Ho, ho, ho"), a song (Coca-Cola's "Teach the World To Sing") or a short jingle (Campbell Soup's "Mmm-mmm-good.")

4. Feel. The general atmosphere of the campaign. Perfume advertising, for example, is known for its attention to feel – some perfumes have a "sexy" feel (i.e., Calvin Klein's Obsession, with its images of sweaty, bare torsos) while others have a cheery, uplifting feel (Clinique's "Happy"). The feel starts with the name and extends to the sense of the advertising.

The Successful Ad Campaign

Every brand and advertising campaign promises something – convenience, longer life, a prettier you. To be successful, the brand must deliver on its promise. If the advertising is effective and consumers are persuaded to try the brand, it had better live up to its expectations. Nothing will kill a weak brand more quickly than good advertising. Effective advertising generates high levels of sampling. If Premium Gold doesn't live up to its promise, it'll lose all those potential new customers.

The advertising must be single-minded. The soul of advertising is the big idea. Successful advertising sticks to the key benefit over and over again, simply and directly. Too many copy points (benefits) confuse the consumer.

Once having found an idea that resonates, smart marketers never depart from it. Since 1948, DeBeers has never abandoned the guilt-inducing refrain "A diamond is forever." The endearingly frantic "Energizer Bunny" debuted in 1989 and is still going strong. The "Got Milk?" campaign that debuted in 1993 continues to marry sexy celebrity images with the wholesome goodness of milk, and the result is a phrase that is now a part of our national consciousness. Perhaps the most recent advertising phenomenon, Verizon Wireless's "Can You Hear Me Now?" campaign – which evokes the quality of Verizon's cellular service – has become a national catchphrase.

The advertising campaign must never talk down to the customer. While consumers enjoy being informed and amused, they don't enjoy being patronized. Good advertising never underestimates the intelligence of consumers. It speaks to them, not at them.

Competition often has the salutary effect of sparking creativity, and so AMA charges three creative teams with creating the final product. These teams work independently of each other to come up with the campaign that will be presented to the client. Winning translates into raises, bonuses and promotion. After a week of internal agency presentations, one team has emerged with the winning campaign. The visuals tie into the card's positioning as the preferred travel card and transform Premium Gold into an airplane, a rental car, a hotel awning, a beach blanket and a ski slope. The text reads "Premium Gold. The Go Card!"

The Media Plan

At the same time, media is fashioning its plan for Premium Gold. With a $50 million dollar budget, they have a lot of options. Using the new consumer profile, media services starts on its analysis. There are a host of questions still to be answered. Among them: Does Premium Gold have a seasonality issue? (Is the card used more often during some seasons than others?) If so, more money should be spent during those peak periods. What media should be used and in what proportion? Planning the appropriate media buys depends on the viewing, reading and lifestyle habits of the target audience, how they see themselves and use the card.

Decisions involving purchasing media depend on many things: the size of the budget, the nature of the brand and the target audience. Assuming the budget is somewhat limited, it's far more effective to focus on one or two media forms rather than dilute the entire effort. $50 million may sound like a lot of money, but media, especially television, is expensive.

After reviewing the available options, media devises a plan calling for the bulk of the advertising to run on network television, supplemented by spot television in Premium Gold's top 10 markets and cable with shows on the Travel Channel. Television advertising accounts for 70 percent of the budget. The remainder will be spent on advertising in travel and general interest magazines (20 percent of the budget), and out-of-home (10 percent of the budget). Additionally, weekly travel specials will be promoted on the card's web site.

The Role of Subsidiaries

The agency's subsidiaries have been on the job as well. AMA Direct has created a continuity travel club program, the "Premium Gold Go Club," awarding cardholders points for card usage transferable for airline, car rental and hotel stays. AMA Promotion has created the "Premium Gold Go Anywhere in the World" instant win sweepstakes. Every time the card is used, the cardholder has the chance to win a free trip anywhere in the world. AMA Public Relations has devised a plan aimed at magazine and newspaper travel writers to announce the campaign.

The Presentation

The presentation is held at AMA headquarters in Chicago. Six agencies will present over two days. Attending for the agency: the president, the media director, the creative director, the head of account planning and the heads of the promotion, direct response and public relations agencies. The agency has two hours to make its case – 90 minutes for the presentation and 30 minutes for discussion. All the materials are brought into the conference room and the A/V equipment is checked and re-checked. The Premium Gold team, including the chairman, marketing director and other executives, files in. Introductions are made and the presentation begins with a combination of PowerPoint slides and ads posted on the walls. Each member of the team presents his or her work. The Premium Gold team interrupts with occasional questions, but it's nothing that AMA can't handle. At the end of the allotted time, AMA is informed that a decision will be made in two weeks.

The AMA team returns to its offices and conducts a post mortem meeting to discuss the presentation and everyone's role in it. The president congratulates everyone on a job well done. Two weeks later, the president's telephone rings. It's Premium Gold's marketing director. AMA has won the competition! Phone calls are made to the team leaders. An inter-office memo is written and immediately distributed to agency employees. Champagne is ordered, a press release is distributed and a party breaks out. The party lasts an hour. Then it's time for the agency's chief financial officer to negotiate a fee with the new client.

The fee is based on the projected number of hours the personnel assigned to the account are projected to work over the next 12 months. Typically, the hours are derived from each individual's salary and then marked up to cover costs, overhead and profit. Compensation agreements tend to vary from client to client, but usually consist of these project fees and media commissions, if the agency will be preparing the media plan for the client as well. Once the fee is set, the real work begins.

Professional Profiles

CHAPTER 5

To give you a better feel for the day-to-day life of professionals in advertising, let's take a closer look at some ad professionals.

Account Services

"I was a double major – business and psychology – at Saint Mary's College in northern California and I knew nothing about business," says Kira Siler, an account executive at Rubin Postaer in Los Angeles. She considered the possibility of becoming a therapist, but decided to take some time off after graduation and moved to Los Angeles.

Like so many others who wandered into the industry, Kira's move to Los Angeles was serendipitous. "My cousin was dating someone whose best friend worked at a major advertising agency and told me about a possible job as an account coordinator on the Mattel account. I interviewed and was hired for the grand salary of $22,000 a year. It didn't take too much time to realize that advertising fit my background perfectly. It's a wonderful combination of business, psychology and entertainment. I worked for a vice president group director. In your first job, you need someone to believe in you, and he did. The work was hard at first. If I left the office at seven in the evening I considered it an early day. But things worked out and within a year I was promoted to assistant account executive.

"I wanted to learn more about advertising so I enrolled in an American Association of Advertising Agencies class on new business pitches. It was terrific! The class was composed of media and account people at the assistant account executive level. We were divided into six teams and had to create a media plan and present it to a panel of judges.

"About a year later I was promoted to account executive. Although working on Mattel at Foote Cone & Belding was a good learning experience, I was very impressed with the work Rubin Postaer had done with Honda and when the opportunity arose I jumped at it. It was a lateral move – I'm an account executive on Acura – but I think a good one. It allowed me to work in a new category, automotive, and I'm enjoying it.

"I'm generally at my desk at 8:30 or 9 in the morning. The first thing I do is check my e-mail and phone messages. The e-mail and messages translate into work, either from the client or other agency departments. I try to devote as much of the morning to meeting with the various agency groups working on my account. If they have any problems or need information or further clarification on the projects they're working on, I get them answers. The first meeting is usually with traffic to determine the status of the ads that are either in development or production. We go over the schedules and check the deadlines to make sure that the work is flowing as it should. The last thing that I want is a surprise.

"After that, I generally meet with media and creative just to see how things are going and answer any questions or ferret out any problems they might have. Right now I'm off to a meeting with the account planner assigned to Acura to review some new information about the brand's corporate targets.

"A good part of my day is reacting to little things – checking the colors of a brochure ready to go to press, getting information, whatever. Right now I'm working on several projects. One is the Collegiate Women's Sports Award, sponsored by Honda, that honors the top women collegiate athletes in the country. The target is college students and I'm working with media to decide the best medium to reach them. I'm also working on the press conference for the project and preparing a creative brief for the award. Budgeting is one of my responsibilities and I've just released the fiscal year 2003 budget and I am working on fiscal year 2004.

"The third project is very exciting. It's a brochure for the Honda Civic GX, a car that runs solely on natural gas, with virtually no emissions.

"My plate is usually full. I see the client once or twice a week. That always generates a conference report and almost always generates work and, of course, there's the occasional shoot to attend. Friends outside of the business think attending a shoot is glamorous, but it's anything but. It is mostly waiting for the ad to be set up.

"I love advertising. It's exactly what I wanted. It gives me all the social and intellectual fulfillment I hoped for. It taught me about business. I not only get to learn about advertising, I learn my client's business as well, and that's the beauty of it. Every day is new, a different learning experience. What really attracts me to the business is the people. They're bright and witty, and their attitude is loose. The business is very social, with lots of young people, and you want to hang with them. I guess that it's a 'don't take yourself too seriously' attitude that separates people in this industry from people outside the business. You can see it at parties and social functions. Somehow, advertising people just sparkle!

"I guess that I can sum up my experience in the business this way: If you love what you do, you'll never work a day in your life."

Creative

"I tried a lot of majors at Syracuse – psychology, communications, TV, radio and film – before I settled on advertising as a major," says Scott Bassin, vice president and associate creative director at Deutsch, in New York. "I originally studied graphic design at Syracuse, but my friends outside of the art school seemed to be having more fun. I chose advertising because I always liked drawing, making stuff and seeing it hanging on my mother and grandmother's fridge. As a kid, I recall being entranced by billboards and I thought that it would be cool to draw them.

"During my junior year, I sent letters to a bunch of creative boutique agencies trying to get an internship. The letters produced an internship at Deutsch Direct, and a neighbor helped me land another internship at BBDO in its marketing science division, where they did market modeling. My bosses were understanding and they allowed me to work a split schedule – three days at one agency, and two days at another. I discovered early on that I didn't like entering data on a spreadsheet and I didn't much care for account management. In my downtime I hung out in the creative area.

"During my senior year, I went back to Syracuse's art school, minored in advertising design and put together a portfolio. After graduation, I made the rounds of the agencies showing my portfolio. After the tenth creative person told me to work on my book, I figured that I had better find something. I didn't want to go back to art school, so I took a nonpaid internship in Deutsch's creative department. They gave me a desk stuck in a small space and I assisted the art directors. I was basically a gofer and I wasn't getting any assignments to improve my portfolio. I decided that I would make my own assignments. I pored through the awards books and picked out brands to create advertising for. My bosses gave me direction and I had all of Deutsch's facilities at my fingertips. It was better than art school. It took a year until I had what I thought was a good portfolio.

I made the rounds of the agencies again, but instead of telling me to go back and work on my stuff, they told me to stay in touch. It was a major breakthrough. With each interview I asked for referrals. I looked for a job for six months but came up dry. I did a little freelance, but it wasn't paying the bills, so I took a job at an art supply store selling portfolios, if you can believe it, and talking to everyone who walked in the door. One of the people I met was a copywriter, David Rosen, who is now my partner. I finally landed an assistant art director job and I was lucky enough to work for Sam Golisano, the creative director. Apparently, he had seen my work before I walked in the door and wanted to hire me. He made a deal with me. I would assist him and he would give me my own work, under his direction. 'Prove that you can do it and I'll promote you!' Six months later he kept his word, and they partnered me with a newly hired copywriter, David Rosen, who I had met selling portfolios. We spent five years working on AT&T, Citibank and Fila. We did a freelance assignment for Equinox Health Clubs that got a lot of notice in the industry and that led to a brief stint at Ammirati & Puris working on Burger King. And then Deutsch came calling.

"We've spent four good years here. We created the campaign for Snapple, 'Personified Bottles.' It ran on MTV, VH1 and Nickelodeon, among others. In the spots, the bottles ran with the bulls – actually guinea pigs – in Pamplona, Spain, hosted a barbeque party and a wedding, performed a synchronized swim routine, frolicked in a bouncing car and took part in a yard sale. The spots were aimed at the 18-24 demographic target.

"Our day usually starts at 9:30 a.m. or 10 a.m. We answer e-mail and phone calls and then it's time to get to work. What we do really depends on whether we're in concept, development or production. We get a cup of coffee, get out the sketch and notepads, close the door, and one of us will say 'Let's work!' We look at the creative strategy brief, and one of us will ask 'What did you do last night?' And we're off and running. The conversation transitions to the work and we start tossing ideas around. Good or bad, nothing's edited until we get a spark, even if it's a bad idea. Then it's time for lunch and we pick up a sandwich and bring it back to the office, check e-mail and phone messages, and it's back to work. That's normally how it works, but sometimes there's a pitch, a client presentation, and everyone's panicking and you get kind of caught up in it.

"There are a couple of things I like about the advertising business. I like deciding how and when you want to work. Nobody cares how you get there, as long as you get there. And I like making stuff – film, photography, music. The thing I like most is having fun and getting people to react to our work."

Media

"I was a sociology major at the University of Hartford, and advertising was the furthest thing from my mind," says Robin Abrutyn, formerly a spot broadcast buyer at Ogilvy & Mather in New York, and Trahan Burden & Charles in Baltimore. "I interviewed for a series of jobs in social work, but I didn't really see a fit. All of my friends were looking for jobs, and one mentioned that she had applied for a job in the media department of an advertising agency. It spurred my curiosity. Before the summer of my junior year I applied for and got an internship at New York's PBS television station, and I really enjoyed it. Working at PBS was some media experience, I thought. I did some research and it seemed that media would be interesting. I prepared for the interview by reading David Ogilvy's *Confessions of an Advertising Man*. I was sold. I applied for a job at Ogilvy, had a zillion interviews and was hired as a media assistant. There is no question that the PBS internship gave me a definite edge over my competition.

What appealed to me most about Ogilvy was that everything that I had read about the company stressed its commitment to, and investment in, training. I had never taken any course remotely associated with advertising or marketing in college, and training was exactly what I needed. The salary was $17,000 and I was glad to get it. After about a month, I entered the media training program. Not only did we learn about media, but I also began to get an understanding of how an agency worked. After six months as an assistant, my supervisor sat me down for an evaluation. I dreaded it, but apparently it went well. I was promoted to media buyer.

"Ogilvy spot media buyers are market specialists and buy media for all agency clients in their markets. It was my job to learn everything about radio and television in the seventeen markets I was assigned. We had to know their programming, audiences, market rank and just about everything else. That's what fascinated me about media. Media is like a giant jigsaw puzzle. There are so many options and buyers have to make educated guesses. We have to put the pieces together based on past performance of the programs we're buying and we don't know if we're right until we do an analysis after the fact.

A typical negotiation goes like this: Based on a variety of market forces, including supply and demand, the program's rating history, competition in the time slot, seasonality and the station's rank in the market, I prepare an estimate of the show's cost per rating point – the cost of reaching one percent of the market population – and multiply by the number rating I expect the show to do. So, if I was buying *Friends* at 8 p.m. in Milwaukee and I estimated that the cost per point was $100 dollars and I expected the show to do an 8 rating, the maximum I would pay would be $800 dollars each time the show runs on my schedule. As in any negotiation, the seller, the station in this case, has a far different view of the world, and is asking $1,000 per spot. My job is to bring that cost down and I do it through negotiation. My client relies on me to get value for money. If I don't, then I'm not a very good buyer. I won more often then I lost because my budgets were generally large for the various clients I bought for and that gave me leverage with the station. We're entrusted with a great deal of money and we treat every dollar as if it was our own.

"After three years, I moved to Baltimore to join Trahan Burden & Charles to work on Harrah's, McCormick and the Maryland State Lottery. It was the first time I had worked outside of New York and I thoroughly enjoyed myself. A significant part of my job was creating and scheduling promotions with the local radio stations. Promotion is usually a part of any radio buy, if the budget is significant. Coca-Cola Enterprises heard of me and recruited me as a marketing services manager.

"It was the right career move, but nothing can compare to the hustle and bustle of an agency. The people I worked with were young, smart and fun to be with. I joined Ogilvy's softball team, attended media parties and tended to hang out after hours with the people I worked with. The thing I loved about working in advertising was that every day was different.

"On a typical day I would arrive at 8:30 or 9 and never leave before 6:30. As I said, we bought spot broadcast for every agency client, and buys would come raining down the minute I got to my desk. I was the queen of multi-tasking! I would be provided with dayparts [a portion of the day on broadcast media, which determines the cost of advertising], flights, client, product, target and budget. Then I had to I call this data into the media representatives of each station in the markets. They got back to me with availabilities, ratings and costs. Using Nielsen and other data, media buyers estimate their own ratings and costs per rating point, and they're always lower than the station's estimates. At that point, we're into a negotiation that can become very spirited. Multiply this by as many as six clients buying the same markets at the same time and you have a very full day."

Media Parties

In any given week, invitations from networks, television and radio stations, magazines and newspapers arrive in people's in-boxes at agencies all over the country. These fetes can range from small intimate affairs to major blowouts with live entertainment and food galore. It's good to be in media when the networks announce their new fall line-ups. In 2003, ABC held its gala at the Radio City Music Hall, CBS took over Carnegie Hall, NBC booked Lincoln Center, and Fox strode the boards at City Center.

GETTING HIRED

Advertising Job Search Basics

CHAPTER 6

According to a recent National Public Radio report quoting the Bureau of Labor Statistics, jobs in advertising have dwindled by 25 percent since 2000. While a turnaround may be on the horizon, you still need every edge you can get.

Preparing For a Career In Advertising

The great thing about the advertising industry is that there is more than one way to break in. The bad thing about advertising is that there is no specific roadmap to follow to get your foot in the door, and you are competing with quite a few other people who are all vying for the same opportunity to break into the industry. You have to be persistent and leave no stone unturned, because there are opportunities – you just have to make them.

Each agency has its own culture, and usually has its own way of starting people out in the business. A relatively common policy at smaller creative boutiques is to start everyone as an administrative assistant first. This lets them get a sense of your talents, and allows you to see where you'd really like to go. The downside, of course, is that the work can be boring. The upside is that you tend to be promoted rather quickly (many times within six months).

Larger agencies tend to have formal training programs that rotate you through a number of departments to see where you fit in, and with whom you "click." These programs are very structured, very competitive and great training. WPP Group, for example, offers a three-year fellowship to give a lucky few the chance to work across different disciplines in any of the agencies within the WPP family (Ogilvy & Mather and J. Walter Thompson, to name two). You can find information about specific job openings on agency websites such as J. Walter Thompson, BBDO, Leo Burnett and Fallon Worldwide. Some large agencies recruit on campus – although this is the exception rather than the rule. (You've got a better shot if you go to school in New York City or at a very top school.) Finally, no matter what the policy or culture, if a friend or a contact within the agency recommends you and you effectively use your network of contacts (more on that to follow), you have a great shot at landing a job.

Selling Yourself in the Ad Market

Landing a job is a matter of luck and timing, especially in a tough economy. You need a plan for packaging yourself and it starts when you're in school, even if you have no career goal. The best way to maximize your chances is to position yourself to match up with a prospective employer and grab the opportunity when it arises. What kinds of employees are advertising agencies looking for? Smart, well-rounded, passionate, likeable, high energy self-starters, with an ability to write and speak clearly and persuasively, and a demonstrated capacity to learn and to grow. Let's examine each characteristic a little more closely.

Smart

In this context, "smart" is shorthand for finely honed common sense. So much of advertising is creative problem solving. It's recognizing that, at the end of the day, it's not about what marketers want to sell. It is about what consumers want to buy. Genius? Hardly. Just plain old common sense. A very long time ago a slim little book, *Obvious Adams*, was published. It was part of every new employee "welcome kit" at Ogilvy & Mather, and required reading. It recounted the story of a young boy of humble origins named Adams who joined a particular company at the lowest entry level and went on to fame and fortune. When asked the reason for his success he responded that, the solutions to the problems that he encountered throughout his career were... obvious! The moral of this story: Genius is fine, smart is better.

When you interview, find something that you have done in a job or at school to highlight your practical smarts. Perhaps you recognized a "hole in the market" that led you into an entrepreneurial business, or there was some extracurricular activity that required your particular brand of creative thinking. Use plenty of examples.

Well-rounded

Many colleges and universities tout their "hot" advertising and communications programs as a way to gain entry into the business. True, there are some schools with very good programs, including the University of Texas, Syracuse and the University of Florida. The real question is: Do these programs offer significant value in landing a job? Probably not. While college-level advertising, marketing and communications courses provide a good theoretical introduction to the industry, they really don't prepare you for the real world of advertising. It can't hurt to take advertising courses, if they're available. Who knows – you might learn that you hate advertising. Better to learn that fact sooner rather than later.

But a traditional liberal arts education is the best preparation for an advertising career, as advertising is about ideas and nothing prepares you for the world of ideas like a solid liberal arts background. The more you know about art, literature, history and psychology, the more prepared you will be to shape ideas to sell brands.

Passionate

Passion, as defined here, is boundless enthusiasm and love for advertising. Advertising is a business, and as in any business there's a degree of drudgery – paperwork, meetings, endless schedules and due dates. But advertising offers one saving grace: the excitement of ideas. And that's where passion struts its stuff. The best place to see it is in a brainstorming session. Ideas fly around and everyone, from the most senior to the most junior person, participates. It's not about titles, it's about ideas. As quickly as they're tacked up on the wall ideas are shot down, until one emerges that has promise. Then that idea is polished like a diamond – and becomes an effective advertisement.

Likeable

In many ways likeability is the most important characteristic employers look for. Generally, you will be competing against applicants as smart, as educated and maybe as passionate as you. Consciously or subconsciously, one of the first factors prospective employers consider when building or adding to a team is whether they want to spend upwards of 12 hours a day with you.

High energy self-starters

"You're not expected to whirl around the office like a dervish, but you are expected to have a 'can do' attitude," says Tim Sickinger, former head of Bozell in Omaha. "The workday is incredibly full and you just don't have time for people who spend their time moping around. You've got to have confidence in your people to step up to the plate without micromanaging every detail." Advertising agencies accept mistakes. When they hire self-starters, mistakes are part and parcel of the learning process and a cost of doing business. However, agencies do have problems paying for the same mistake twice.

Communicators

An often heard lament among advertising professional is that good writing and speaking is becoming a lost art. Advertising is a communications discipline and requires its practitioners to write and speak in easily understood English. "I was fresh out of Radcliffe when I started work at Ogilvy & Mather as an assistant account executive, and I have to admit that

I was pretty full of myself," says Jody Cukier, who now runs her own consulting business. "My first project was to write a rather long conference report. I dashed it off in a half an hour and gave it to my boss to review before I distributed it. An hour later it was back on my desk with more arrows and crossouts than I thought possible. The whole thing had to be redone. To add insult to injury there was a big red "D" in the upper right hand corner. My first reaction was anger, but when I re-read his comments I realized that he was right. Simple declarative sentences are a lot better than complicated gibberish."

Capacity to learn and grow

David Ogilvy once described advertising as the only business where the company's assets go down on the elevator every night. It is in an agency's interest to hire smart people and tend to their growth as if they were rare breeds of orchids. Stories of people hired in the most junior positions and rising to top agency management positions are not apocryphal. Cream rises to the top as a result of hard work and dedication. It happens all the time, in every department. Every day on the job is a new learning experience. Does luck play a part in getting hired or promoted? Sure. But smart people make their own luck.

The Value of an MBA

Will an MBA help you get a job in advertising? Advertising pros aren't enamored with the degree. "I don't think that the MBA adds a whole lot," says Pen Pendleton of Rubin Postaer. "We hire smart people who love advertising and train them." Another ad professional echoes this view. "In my experience, MBAs come to the party with a boatload of preconceived notions – theories – about the business and it takes some time to knock it out of them. Advertising is a very practical business, more about people and less about theory." An MBA may help you get an advertising job based on networking alone. But before you go heavily into debt, work in the business for a few years, and then decide.

The Importance of Internships

An internship is basically an eight- to 12-week apprenticeship offering a taste of real work experience, resume value and the possibility of getting hired upon graduation. Summer internships, full- and part-time, paid and nonpaid, are available at a variety of communications companies. Most major advertising agencies offer internships, as do sales promotion, public relations and direct response agencies, local radio and television stations, magazines and even television networks. Employers view interns as cheap, temporary labor on special projects, and as candidates for future employment.

"During the summer of my junior year at the University of Wisconsin at Madison, I was fortunate enough to land an internship at CBS Network News, and without a doubt it was a great experience," says Dan Berkowitz. "I was a political science major with no real career direction, but working on documentaries at CBS really started me on my career in advertising and marketing. Sure, there was a lot of what I thought was meaningless scut work – juggling paper, trafficking materials and running errands – but I got to work with some really bright people. And I got to put something on a resume besides my counselor and lifeguard jobs. There's no doubt in my mind that the internship helped me land a job."

At advertising agencies, interns work in virtually every department.

Account management: Supervised by one or more account executives, interns help keep the budget, coordinate creative and research activities, and follow up with suppliers.

Creative: Copy and art interns get a chance to observe the creative process and do a limited amount of writing and art direction under the supervision of copywriters and art directors.

Media: Interns work under buying and planning supervisors gathering and analyzing viewership, circulation and demographic data for all media forms.

Research: Interns are generally assigned to specific projects for data gathering and limited analysis.

Production (print and broadcast): Interns begin to learn the production process and work with outside suppliers in a follow-up capacity.

Here are some productive strategies for securing an internship:

- Contact the American Association of Advertising Agencies (AAAA) and your local advertising club.
- The Dow Jones Newspaper Fund sponsors summer internships in advertising at daily newspapers throughout the United States. (www.dowjones.com/careers/internships/index.html
- *Salon* provides a database of internships with magazines, new media, broadcast and newspapers. (www.salon.com)
- Magazine Publishers of America lists a variety of magazine internships. (www.magazine.org/internships/)

Networking

Networking is the process of actively establishing contacts with people who may help you get a job now and in the future. It is also the best way to find those jobs that are unadvertised

Whether finding an internship or your first, second or even third job, networking should be a key element of your plan. Many advertising jobs come as a result of referrals or personal recommendations. A personal recommendation or a referral carries more weight than a "casting call." How do you find these jobs? By regarding every contact with another person who has crossed your path, however briefly, a networking opportunity.

Ten Tips For Effective Networking

First, identify your network (target audience). "But I don't know a lot of people," you say. Sure you do. You just haven't taken the time to think about it.

Now, buy a small three-ring binder with tabs – it will be your bible – and devote a section to each category of contact. If you're more comfortable using your computer, by all means do. Under each category, list the names, telephone numbers and addresses – if you have them – of each contact. You'll find that networking is a process of elimination. Keep the productive contacts and discard the others. That way you'll always be up-to-date. Update your network bible weekly for as long as you live and it will prove to be the most valuable book you will ever own.

1. **Identify where to network.** First, tap your family and friends (and your friends' families.) But other resources can be just as valuable.

Local advertising clubs: The American Advertising Federation lists over 200 advertising clubs in small and large markets throughout the United States. These clubs are perfect venues for networking, information gathering and internships. The New York Advertising Club, for example offers a special internship program, and other local clubs have similar programs.

Alumni associations: These are a goldmine of networking opportunities. Every college and university keeps meticulous records of its graduates and their accomplishments are usually noted in alumni publications. The college library keeps back issues on file. Use them. Also, most colleges and universities have alumni clubs scattered around the country. Dues are minimal but the rewards can be great.

Fraternities and sororities: The party's over! Welcome to the real world. This is where four years of dues pay off. It's one thing to be an alumnus of a college attempting to network with other alumni. It's an entirely different matter to be members of the same sorority or fraternity, sisters and brothers. Fraternities and sororities are an existing network. Tap into it.

Local politicians: You probably don't know your senator, congressman, assemblyman or state senator, but they know a lot of people. Important people. "Yeah, but why should they bother with me?" you ask. The answer might surprise you: You're a voter and an important member of a family of voters. If you're looking for a job during an election year, it's even better. Volunteer to work with your representative's communications staff, or with the agency if he or she has one. If you're good, you'll catch someone's eye and add important people to your network. You've also gained valuable, relevant communications experience to put on your resume.

2. **Remember that you're a product.** Use the tools of advertising to create a 60-second commercial about you. It begins with the creative strategy statement.

Objective – what must advertising accomplish?

Target audience – who is the customer?

Key benefit – why should the customer buy the product?

Support – why should the customer believe the benefit?

Tone and manner – what is the product's personality?

What's your objective? A job obviously, but specifically what job? Media? Research? Account Services? Who's the target audience? Make a list of the companies you would like to work for. Why should they hire you (key benefit)? "I've always wanted to be in advertising," "I'm really creative," or "advertising seems like fun," just won't cut it. Be clear about the points that support your candidacy. And when you're all done with the strategy statement, write a brief ad about you. Edit mercilessly until you get to the one key reason why you would be perfect for the job, and then memorize and rehearse it until you have it down pat.

3. Pop the question. With family and friends it's easy. They know you're looking for a job, but with casual acquaintances or friends of friends, or even total strangers, it's a little bit different. Remember, everyone you meet is a potential conduit into the industry. Errant conversations with seatmates on airplanes can turn into interviews and jobs. Size the prospect up and learn to steer the conversation toward careers. Conversations about nothing often lead to something. A simple "What do you do for a living?" is a perfect qualifier. Once you determine that they know someone who works in the industry, or are in the industry themselves, rather than thrust a resume into their hands – an instant turn off – explain that you're thinking about working in advertising and merely gathering information. You're not asking them to get you a job, just an informational interview. This approach usually works like a charm. You're selling them *you*, and they don't even realize it.

4. Research your target companies. When you do interview, whether it's for a real job or just an informational interview, be prepared. You will most certainly be asked about what interested you in the company. The more you know about the company, the better off you'll be. Every library has the *Standard Directory of Advertising Agencies*, also known as "The Red Book." The Red Book lists every agency in the United States, their clients, billings and key personnel. To get a sense of the agency's philosophy, services and examples of recent campaigns and case histories, visit the agency's web site.

5. **Demonstrate a love for advertising.** Using the Red Book, research the company's clients and determine the commercials they're running. Become knowledgeable about those commercials. Form an educated opinion about them. Compare them with other commercials in the category. Be prepared to discuss them with the folks you will be interviewing with.

6. **Make friends**. A common mistake networkers make is treating the contact as, well, a contact. They couldn't be more wrong! Every contact is a potential friend. Let's say you call your Aunt Edith, whom you haven't spoken to in 13 years, but she's in your network database under "Family," and it turns out that she plays bridge with the wife of a management supervisor at Acme Advertising. She offers to ask her bridge partner if it's all right for you to call her husband. A few days later Aunt Edith calls back with the wonderful news. The management supervisor will see you. What do you do? You call and make an appointment for an informational interview, but how do you handle it? By making a new friend. Presumably, you've done the research, you know all about the agency, its clients and its philosophy. You've memorized and rehearsed your one-minute commercial about you until it fits like a second skin. Now you're ready.

After exchanging pleasantries, you explain that you're there for information about career opportunities in advertising and ask for any insights and advice he may have. Then you keep quiet and let him talk. It's human nature that no matter the business, people love to talk about themselves! Do look for an opportunity to deliver your one-minute commercial, and look for any area of common ground. Don't ask for a job; let the conversation move in that direction. If it doesn't, politely ask if he knows of anyone else you might talk with. More often then not, he'll refer you to a colleague in another company, and then you will have a new addition to your network

7. **Follow up**. Always follow up after an interview with a short thank-you note. Reference the advice and insights you received and don't forget to mention how helpful the experience was. Flattery goes a long way, but don't lay it on too thick. Be professional. Besides, you never know if in a week or a month an opportunity may arise and you, the brand, could be considered. One other point: If you intend to use the contact's name with another company, always get permission first.

8. **Stay in touch**. Friends keep in touch. Keep your network active by the occasional contact. Perhaps it's a magazine article you've read that

might be of interest, or a new book on some facet of advertising that you think some of your contacts might enjoy. Keep them aware of you.

9. **Keep meticulous records.** After each interview, record the highlights of the meeting. This will prevent embarrassing situations and keep you from looking stupid in subsequent conversations your new "friend" referred you to.

10. **Always remember that you reap what you sow.** Networking is a two-way street. One day, you're going to be in a position to help someone who helped you when you needed it, or someone who just needs your help. There's an old expression that is particularly apt: "Top dog today, bottom dog tomorrow!" You will be treated as you treat others. Advertising is a relatively small and close-knit industry. There are good guys and bad guys, and word travels fast.

Sample Networking Letter

Top advertising executives are busy. Here's an example of a good networking letter you might write to follow up on a hot lead. You can also e-mail networking letters. Always err on the side of formality.

Ms. Susan Smith
Vice President Account Director
Acme Advertising
1234 Madison Avenue
New York, NY 10502

Dear Ms. Smith:

Bob Randall, senior vice president of media at Jones Advertising, suggested that I write to you. I met with him recently to talk about media as a possible career option and he was very helpful. He suggested that you might be able to provide some insight into the opportunities in account services.

I am a senior at New York University majoring in English literature. My interest in an advertising career is a result of work I did as a volunteer on Senator Hillary Clinton's election campaign and my subsequent internship at Jack Morris Advertising.

I would like a few minutes of your time to explore the role of account services, what a typical day is like, the kinds of problems you encounter and the most rewarding part of your job.

I know your time is valuable. I will call next week to arrange a brief meeting.

Sincerely,

Jane Smart

Resumes, Cover Letters, Interviews and Portfolios

CHAPTER 7

Creating a Killer Resume

A resume is a shorthand recitation of accomplishments, not jobs. It's also a selling document designed to accomplish three things:

- Get prospective employers to think about you in a particular way
- Convince them that you will bring value to their business
- Whet their appetite and lead to an interview

Advertising resumes should focus on creative problem solving. Even if your job experience falls into the camp counselor/lifeguard category, find one or two examples of how you were faced with a problem and solved it.

Here are some overall suggestions relative to your resume's look, feel and tone.

- **One page should do the trick.** Resumes aren't narratives. They're tight summaries designed for easy reading. Agencies receive hundreds of resumes a week and busy people have to read them. Make it easy on your audience and keep it short.
- **Keep it pertinent.** In a one-page resume, words are at a premium. Every entry relative to skills, ability and achievement should support your job objective. For example, let's say that you studied abroad during your junior year and traveled through Europe. One way to turn this into an advantage is to position yourself as someone who's a student of human behavior and curious about how different cultures influence behavior.
- **Use action words.** Use the active voice to sell. Words like "led," "managed," "designed," "convinced," "involved" and "created" add zing to the resume and position you as someone who gets things done.
- **Avoid fluff.** Steer clear of colored paper, word art, trendy typefaces and cutesy layouts. The reader will not be impressed. Choose a professional-looking, easy-to-read layout and typeface. Times New Roman is always a good bet.

- **Proofread your resume.** Poor grammar will lead your resume directly to the circular file. Make sure you proofread and spell check your resume, and give it to trusted friends to look over for good measure.

A Closer Look at Each Resume Section

Heading

Be sure to include your name, current address if you're a student, home address, telephone numbers and e-mail address.

Job objective

Be very clear and concise. "Assistant Art Director," "Account Executive," "Media Planner." Avoid flabby, imprecise statements like "I would like to use my creative abilities in an entry-level position at your agency." If you can't be specific, leave the objective out.

Work experience

This is the most important part of your resume. In this section you can turn flax into gold. "Work experience" includes jobs, internships, summer employment, volunteer work or anything else that remotely qualifies as work, either paid or unpaid. List your jobs and dates of employment in reverse chronological order, your last job first. Using action words, describe your accomplishments in detail. Demonstrate leadership, problem solving, initiative and the results. Did you go beyond your assigned responsibilities? Were you involved in training? Were you required to write or analyze anything?

Education

List your college, your major, the degree and any honors you may have received.

Computer skills

A job in advertising requires skills with programs like Windows, Word, Excel and PowerPoint. If you are interested in landing a job in the creative area, it's quickly becoming a requirement that you know Quark, Illustrator and

Photoshop as well. If you don't have experience with these programs, make plans to get some training. (Enroll in a weekend course or find a tutor to teach you the basics).

Language skills

If you're proficient in one or more foreign languages, include it in this section. Many agencies have offices throughout the world, so language skills are an advantage.

Interests and activities

In this section, prospective employers learn about your personal side. Professional organizations, athletics, charitable work and other similar activities belong here. Never include personal data like height, weight or age.

Tips On Mailing Your Resume

- Use a standard business envelope. Your resume will get a higher response.
- Mail your resume at the beginning of the week. It will arrive toward the end of the week when there is less mail volume.
- Handwrite the address on the envelope. Handwritten envelopes get noticed.
- Write a great cover letter.

Sample Resume

Judy Smith

1234 Main Street
New York, NY 10025

Home: (212) 123-4567
Work: (212) 333-6666 ext. 2503
E-mail: jsmith@abc.com

JOB OBJECTIVE

Account supervisor

EMPLOYMENT EXPERIENCE

American Consulting Group; Westport, Connecticut **March 2000 – Present**

Project Manager: Managed multiple marketing consulting engagements in packaged goods and services industries. Clients included Sprint, H.J. Heinz, Pillsbury, Lens Express and United Parcel Service. Functions included:

- Strategic Plan Development: Created a strategic plan for a residential long distance telecommunications provider. Recommendations resulted in the introduction of three new products and a residential long distance market share increase from 6% to 8%.
- Advertising Consolidation: Assessed global advertising agency program for a consumer packaged goods company. Recommendations led to consolidation of the company's advertising agencies and an implementation of a company-wide agency review, compensation and management system.
- Retail: Recommended an overall strategy and implementation plan to address retail market opportunities, product and service capabilities, and organizational structure for a package delivery company. Recommendations lead to a $500 million investment in the retail channel.
- Direct Marketing: Identified alternative product offerings and new channel opportunities for large mail order contact lens provider. Recommendations resulted in the company's acquisition of a health and beauty company.
- Additional Assignments: Managed 10+ consulting assignments in three years.

Big Agency, Inc.; New York, New York **September 1997-February 2000**

- ***Account Executive:*** Developed business-to-business and business-to-consumer marketing programs for the United States Postal Service.
- ***Assistant Account Executive:*** Created business-to-business direct marketing programs for AT&T.

EDUCATION

The University of Wisconsin; Madison, Wisconsin **September 1990-May 1994**

Bachelor of Arts in Political Science, May 1994

PERSONAL

Proficient with Microsoft Word, PowerPoint and Excel. Extensive experience with IRI, Nielsen and ASI.

Creating a Great Cover Letter

It's time to dust off your one-minute commercial again. A cover letter is always sent with a resume and can help get your resume read. The cover letter is the first communication you'll make with a prospective employer. It should be enthusiastic and to the point. You will be judged as much as on your enthusiasm and your background as your ability to communicate.

Overall, your cover letter should:

- Be no more than one page.
- Be business-like in tone.
- Show that you have spent time researching and thinking about the company.
- Be addressed to an individual.
- Express interest in the company.
- Set out your skills and experience, and explain why you would be a perfect fit.

What your cover letter is not is a recapitulation of your resume. Let your personality come through. Let's take a closer, paragraph-by-paragraph look at the cover letter.

Paragraph 1: This is your headline. Be direct. State the job you want, how you heard about it and why you are interested.

Paragraph 2: The one-minute commercial. What is there about your background and experience that qualifies you for the job? Bring in all of your supporting points, examples of initiative, problem solving and leadership. Show how you are equipped to use your skills and abilities to do the job. Make the reader want to read your resume.

Paragraph 3: Show that you've done your homework by demonstrating knowledge of the company.

Paragraph 4: Close the sale by asking for an interview. Thank the reader.

The Creative Portfolio

Creative is the only department that requires concrete, visible talent in its recruits – the ability to conceptualize and turn those concepts into ad writing if you're a copywriter, or ad design if you're an art director. If you're applying for a job in the creative department, in addition to a resume you must have a creative portfolio – examples of your art or copy. Courses in creating portfolios are available for art directors and copywriters at colleges, universities and independent schools. The coursework focuses on creating copy and art in a variety of communication formats including television, radio, print and Internet materials, with the goal of building your portfolio for presentation.

The portfolio is a collection of your best work and is often left with a prospective employer, giving you no opportunity to lovingly describe the contents. Therefore, each piece should have a description attached.

- How many samples? Let common sense be your guide. Ten to 12 is probably enough.
- Get their interest immediately. Always arrange your portfolio with the cleverest or most eye-catching work in the front. First impressions are important.
- If possible, match the work to the agency. Do a little research. Try to match your work to the categories in which the agency's clients are represented. For example, if the agency represents American Airlines, include an ad for an airline – but not American. They know their client intimately and you run the risk of having your work compared to their advertising.
- Invest in a good presentation binder for your work. Binder size should not exceed 26"x 36" (the size of a standard shipping box).
- Stand out from the crowd with a good web site. If your interest is in web design, create your own web site that serves as an online portfolio and highlights the work you've done. It's a good way to stand out from the crowd and gives you more control over how your work is presented. List your URL on your resume, so prospective employers are free to check out your work.

Freelance Temping

One way to land a job in the creative department of an agency is to work as a freelance temp. There are regional temp agencies that specialize in art directors and copywriters, and they place people on specific projects where agencies might need some extra help. The best place to find these is by asking a receptionist at an agency for several recommendations. Some companies to try are Aquent, Buzz Company (www.buzzco.com) and Artisan Creative.

The Interview

What's the advertising interviewer looking for? Several things.

- Confidence that you have the skills to do the job
- A sense that you will be a good fit on the team and in the agency
- Maturity
- Poise
- Enthusiasm
- Promotability
- A love for advertising

Notice that only one characteristic has anything to do with actual competence. The other six relate to you as a person. Interviewers consider it a given that the pool of people they're interviewing are smart and capable. It's the intangibles they really look for. Perhaps you're surprised that the potential for being promoted is an important criterion. Don't be.

Basic Interviewing Tips

- Smile.
- Prepare and rehearse examples of your proudest achievements.
- Take the interviewer's lead. Don't offer more information than requested.
- Be attentive.
- Answer only the question asked.
- If you don't understand the question, ask that it be repeated.
- Give firm handshakes.
- Maintain eye contact.
- Dress professionally.
- First names are out, unless you have permission.
- Bring a pen and extra copies of your resume.

Interviewing Techniques

With the possible exception of human resources professionals, who are often the first interviewers job seekers meet in the hiring process, interviewers at ad agencies are not trained in the art of the interview, so you should expect a wide variety of interview formats. The previous section discussed what interviewers are looking for. This section will show you how to deliver the goods.

STAR

STAR is an acronym for a method of responding to interview questions about challenges you've faced in the past.

S = Situation: The Problem

T = Target: The Goal

A = Action: How You Handled It

R = Results: The Outcome and Lessons Learned

Here's how to use it. An interviewer might ask you to describe how you demonstrated initiative, handled a troublesome boss or convinced a group to follow your lead. STAR provides the framework for you to structure your answer. Interviewers are as interested in your delivery as your solution. They expect you to be articulate, knowledgeable, to the point, and convincing.

Some interviewers take an entirely different approach. They ask questions like, "What was the last book you read?" to get a sense of your personality. (Don't answer with some tome of the advertising field – this just sounds like brown-nosing.) Or they ask confrontational questions, like, "What don't you like about this agency's creative product?" Be honest. If you're new to the business the appropriate answer is that you don't know enough yet to evaluate the agency's work. They're trying to gauge your reaction to the unexpected. Don't get flustered. Answer with logic, humor or wit and honesty and you will win them over. Stick to your guns and don't flipflop – the interviewer is looking for a well-reasoned opinion, not aimless flattery.

Sample Interview Questions

These are some general interview questions you should be prepared to answer.

- Why are you interested in this company?
- What do you know about this company?
- Why did you choose advertising as a career?
- What do think you can bring to (job objective)?
- Tell me about yourself.
- What are your strengths? Weaknesses?
- How would you describe yourself?
- Why should we hire you?
- How do you react to deadlines and pressure?
- What are you most proud of?
- What are your three favorite advertising campaigns and why?
- What was the last book or movie that you read or saw?
- What did you learn from your internships that you could apply here?
- Where do you expect to be in five years?
- Are you interviewing anywhere else?
- Is there anything else I should know about you?

Questions For the Interviewer

- What skills are you looking for?
- How is the department organized?
- Is this a new position? If not, what happened to the person who previously filled it?
- What objectives have you set for this job?
- What's a typical day like?
- What do you enjoy about your work?
- How are the agency's relations with its clients?
- Describe the corporate culture.
- Is there a training program?
- Do you have a formal evaluation system?
- What is the single most important thing you need done over the next three months?
- What brand will I be working on?
- What are the brand's most pressing problems?
- What is the typical career path?
- When may I expect to hear from you?

Thank You Notes

Always send a thank you note the day after the interview. The note should refer to the date and time of the interview, the job you interviewed for, how grateful you are that they saw you and convey a clear expression of your continuing interest and qualifications for the job. If there was some additional information your interviewer requested, include it. If you had multiple interviews at the same company, each interviewer should receive a thank you note, tailored specifically for each. Use attractive stationery.

APPENDIX

Industry Organizations

American Association of Advertising
666 Third Avenue
New York, NY 10017
Phone: (212) 682-2500

Advertising Women of New York
153 East 57th Street
New York, NY 10022
Phone: (212) 593-1950

The Advertising Research Foundation
641 Lexington Avenue
New York, NY 10022
Phone: (212) 751-5656

American Advertising Federation
1225 Connecticut Avenue NW
Washington, DC 20036
Phone: 1-800-999-2331

Magazines

Advertising Age
Television Editorial Corp.
1270 Avenue of the Americas
New York, NY 10020
Phone: (212) 757-8400
www.adage.com

Crain Communications
740 Rush Street
Chicago, IL 60611
Phone: 1-800-678-9595
www.crains.com

Crains publishes a variety of trade magazines that you might find useful, like *Television Week*, *Creativity* and others.

Adweek
ASM Communications
P.O. Box 1974
Danbury, CT 06813
Phone: 1-800-722-6658
www.adweek.com

Brandweek
ASM Communications
P.O. Box 1974
Danbury, CT 06813
Phone: 1-800-722-6658
www.brandweek.com

Communication Arts
110 Constitution Drive
Menlo Park, CA 94025
www.commarts.com

Interesting Web Sites

MediaWeek – www.mediaweek.com

Promo – www.promomagazine.com
Promo Magazine is aimed at the promotion marketing executive who develops all manner of campaigns for major advertisers.

Direct – www.directmag.com
Aimed at professionals who handle direct marketing campaigns and businesses for their clients – from American Express to Bose to all major packaged goods companies like Procter & Gamble who use direct marketing as part of their overall marketing strategy.

The New York Times – www.nytimes.com
Sign up to receive a free newsletter from Stuart Elliott, the *Times'* major advertising critic and an influential voice in the Advertising Industry. His newsletter often mentions recent promotions and hirings, so you can begin to build a database of people in jobs you'd like to learn more about and contact them directly. You can also see where they left and inquire about recent job openings!

MediaBistro – www.mediabistro.com
MediaBistro offers all the latest job openings in the publishing industry, as well as information for new or established journalists and copywriters.

Recommended Reading

How to Advertise: Third Edition, Kenneth Roman and Jane Maas, Thomas Duane Books, 2003

Ogilvy On Advertising, David Ogilvy, Vintage, 1985.

Madison & Vine, Scott Donaton, McGraw-Hill, 2004.

Creative Advertising: Ideas and Techniques from the World's Best Campaigns, Mario Pricken, Thomas & Hudson, 2002.

The End of Advertising as We Know It, Sergio Zyman with Armin Brott, John Wiley & Sons, 2002.

The Super Bowl of Advertising: How the Commercials Won the Game, Bernice Kanner, Bloomberg Press, 2003.

Ads, Fads, and Consumer Culture: Advertising's Impact on American Character and Society, Arthur Asa Berger, Rowman & Littlield, 2000.

A Big Life in Advertising, Mary Wells Lawrence, Touchstone Books, 2003.

AAF Member Clubs

Alabama

Advertising Federation of Greater Mobile
Birmingham Advertising Federation
Montgomery Advertising Federation
Shoals Advertising Federation
Southeast Alabama Advertising Federation
Tennessee Valley Advertising Federation
Tuscaloosa Advertising Federation

Alaska

Advertising Federation of Alaska

Arizona

Ad 2 Phoenix
Phoenix Advertising Club
Tucson Advertising Club

Arkansas

Arkansas Advertising Federation
Greater Fort Smith Ad Club
Northwest Arkansas Advertising Federation

California

Ad 2 Los Angeles
AdMark! The Bay Area Advertising & Marketing Association
Advertising Club of Los Angeles
Advertising Club of San Diego
Advertising Club of Silicon Valley
Advertising Federation of the Desert
Fresno Advertising Federation
Inland Empire Ad Club
Los Angeles Advertising Women
Orange County Advertising Federation
Sacramento Advertising Club
Ventura County Advertising Club, Inc.

Colorado

Denver Advertising Federation
Pikes Peak Advertising Federation, Inc.

District of Columbia

Advertising Club of Metro Washington

Florida

Ad 2 Miami
Ad 2 Greater Orlando
Ad 2 Tampa Bay
Advertising Federation of the Greater Palm Beaches
Advertising Club of Greater Fort Lauderdale
Advertising Federation of Greater Miami
Advertising Federation of Southwest Florida
Advertising Federation of the Suncoast
Daytona Beach Advertising Federation
Emerald Coast Advertising Federation
Gainesville Advertising Federation
Greater Ocala Advertising Federation
Greater Tallahassee Advertising Federation
Imperial Polk Advertising Federation
Jacksonville Marketing and Advertising Club

Orlando Advertising Federation
Space Coast Advertising Federation
Tampa Bay Advertising Federation
West Florida Advertising Federation

Georgia

Central Georgia Advertising Federation
Advertising Federation of Columbus
Athens Advertising Club
Atlanta Advertising Club
Augusta Advertising Federation
Northeast Georgia Advertising Federation
Savannah Advertising Federation

Hawaii

Ad 2 Honolulu
Hawaii Advertising Federation

Idaho

Boise Advertising Federation
Idaho Falls Advertising Federation

Illinois

Central Illinois Advertising Association
Chicago Advertising Federation
Greater Rockford Advertising Club
Peoria Advertising & Selling Club

Indiana

AdClub Indianapolis
Advertising Club of Evansville
Advertising Club of Michiana
Advertising Federation of East Central Indiana
Advertising Federation of Fort Wayne
Association of Advertising and Marketing Professionals

Iowa

Advertising Club of Dubuque
Advertising Federation of Sioux City
Advertising Federation of Cedar Rapids
Advertising Professionals of Des Moines
Marketing Advertising &
Communications Professionals of NE Iowa
Quad City Advertising Federation

Kansas

Advertising Federation of Wichita
Topeka Advertising Federation

Kentucky

Ad 2 Lexington
Ad 2 Louisville
Advertising Federation of Louisville
Lexington Advertising Club

Louisiana

Acadiana Advertising Federation
Advertising Club of New Orleans
Advertising Club of Northeast Louisiana
Advertising Federation of Greater Baton Rouge
Central Louisiana Advertising Club
Lake Charles Advertising Federation
Shreveport-Bossier Advertising Federation

Maryland

Advertising Association of Baltimore
Greater Frederick Advertising Federation

Massachusetts

The Ad Club (formerly Boston Idea Group)

Michigan

Adcraft Club of Detroit
Ad Club of West Michigan Inc.
Advertising Federation of Saginaw Valley
Ann Arbor Advertising Club
Flint Area Advertising Federation
Lansing Advertising Club, Inc.

Minnesota

Advertising Federation of Minnesota
Central Minnesota Advertising Federation
Lake Superior Advertising Federation

Mississippi

Ad Federation of South Mississippi
Golden Triangle Advertising Federation
Jackson Advertising Federation
Mississippi Delta Advertising Club
Mississippi Gulf Coast Advertising Club

Missouri

Advertising Club of Greater St. Louis
Advertising Club of Kansas City
Joplin Area Advertising Federation
Mid Missouri Advertising Federation
Springfield Advertising Association
Tri-State Advertising and Marketing Club

Montana

Billings Advertising and Marketing Federation
Great Falls Advertising Federation
Helena Advertising Federation
Missoula Advertising & Marketing Federation

Nebraska

Advertising Federation of Lincoln
Omaha Federation of Advertising

Nevada

Advertising Association of Northern Nevada
Las Vegas Advertising Federation

New Mexico

Advertising Federation of Las Cruces
New Mexico Advertising Federation
Santa Fe Advertising Club

New York

Ad Club (Albany)
Advertising Club of New York
Advertising Women of New York
African Americans in Advertising
Brainstorm – The Communicators Club of Buffalo Inc.
Rochester Advertising Federation
Syracuse Advertising Club

North Carolina

Ad Club of the Triad
Ad Club of the Triangle
Charlotte Advertising Club
PACE (Professional Ad Club East)

North Dakota

Advertising Federation of Bismarck-Mandan
Advertising Federation of Fargo-Moorhead

Ohio

Advertising Club of Cincinnati
Advertising Club of Toledo
Advertising Federation of Columbus
Advertising Federation of Greater Akron
Canton Advertising Club
Cleveland Advertising Association
Dayton Advertising Club

Oklahoma

Oklahoma City Advertising Club
Tulsa Advertising Federation

Oregon

Ad 2 Portland
Advertising Federation of Central Oregon
Portland Advertising Federation

Pennsylvania

Advertising Club of Central Pennsylvania
Erie Advertising Club
Lehigh Valley Advertising Club
Northeast Pennsylvania Advertising Club
Philadelphia Advertising Club
Pittsburgh Advertising Federation

South Carolina

Advertising Federation of Charleston
Coastal Advertising & Marketing Professionals
Columbia Advertising Club
Greenville Advertising Club

South Dakota

Black Hills Advertising Federation
South Dakota Advertising Federation

Tennessee

Chattanooga Advertising Federation
Knoxville Advertising Federation
Memphis Advertising Federation
Nashville Advertising Federation
Tri-City Metro Advertising Federation
West Tennessee Advertising Federation

Texas

Abilene Texas Advertising Club
Ad 2 Houston
Advertising Club of Fort Worth
Advertising Club of Waco
Advertising Federation of El Paso
Amarillo Advertising Federation
Austin Advertising Federation
Central Texas Advertising League
Corpus Christi Advertising Federation
Dallas Advertising League
East Texas Advertising Federation
Houston Advertising Federation
Lubbock Advertising Federation
Permian Basin Advertising Federation
San Angelo Advertising Federation
San Antonio Advertising Federation
Southeast Texas Advertising Federation
Texoma Chapter of the American Advertising Federation
Valley Advertising Federation
Victoria Advertising Federation

Utah

Utah Advertising Federation

Virginia

Ad 2 of the Roanoke Valley
Advertising Club of Central Virginia
Advertising Club of Hampton Roads
Advertising Federation of the Roanoke Valley

Washington

Ad 2 Seattle
Seattle Advertising Federation
Spokane Advertising Federation
Yakima Advertising Federation

West Virginia

Advertising Association of Charleston

Wisconsin

Advertising Association of Fox River Valley
Green Bay Advertising Federation
LaCrosse Area Advertising Federation
Madison Advertising Federation

Puerto Rico

Asociacion de Agencias Publicitarias de Puerto Rico

Virgin Islands

Advertising Club of The Virgin Islands
Caribbean Advertising Federation

Advertising Glossary

AAA: American Academy of Advertising. An association comprised of advertising students and educators.

AAAA: American Association of Advertising Agencies. Advertising agency industry association.

ANA: Association of National Advertisers. An association of marketers that advertise their products.

Advertising: The art of building brands using mass media.

Advertising allowance: Money provided by a manufacturer to a retailer or distributor as an incentive to advertise a specific product or brand.

Advertising plan: A detailed outline of what goals an advertising campaign should achieve, how to accomplish them, and how to determine whether or not the campaign was successful.

Advertising research: Research conducted to improve the efficacy of advertising.

Agate line: A measure of newspaper advertising space, one column wide and 1/14th inch deep.

Agency commission: The agency's fee for creating and placing advertisements.

Aided recall: A research method used to determine what consumers remember about an advertisement they have seen or heard.

Answer print: The final edited version of a television commercial.

Arbitron: Television and radio rating service that publishes regular reports for selected markets.

Area of dominant influence (ADI): A geographic designation, used by Arbitron, that specifies which counties fall into a specific television market.

Art proof: The artwork for an ad, to be submitted for client approval.

Artwork: The visual components of an ad, not including the typeset text.

Audience: The total number of people or households exposed to an ad or commercial, and whether they actually saw or heard the ad or commercial.

Audience duplication: The number of people who saw or heard more than one of the programs or publications in which an ad was placed.

Audit Bureau of Circulations (ABC): A company that audits the circulation of print publications to insure that reported circulation figures are accurate.

Availability: Advertising time on radio or television that is available for purchase, at a specific time.

Average audience: The number of homes or people tuned to a television program during an average minute, or the number of people who viewed an average issue of a print publication.

Back to back: Running more than one commercial, with one following immediately after another.

Bait advertising: Advertising a product at a very low price, when it is difficult or even impossible to obtain the product for the price advertised.

Barter: Exchanging merchandise, or something other than money, for advertising time or space.

Ben Day process: A shading or dot pattern on a drawing.

Billboard: (1) An outdoor sign or poster; (2) Sponsor identification at the beginning or end of a television show.

Billings: Total amount charged to clients including the agency commission, media costs, production costs, etc.

Bleed: Allowing a picture or ad to extend beyond the normal margin of a printed page, to the edge of the page.

Boutique: An agency that provides a limited service, such as one that does creative work but does not provide media planning, research, etc. Usually, this refers to a relatively small company.

Brand development index (BDI): A comparison of the percent of a brand's sales in a market to the percent of the national population in that same market.

Brand manager: Individual who has marketing responsibilities for a specific brand.

Brand name: Name used to distinguish a product from its competitors.

Business-to-business advertising: Advertising directed to other businesses rather than to consumers.

Camera-ready art: Artwork that is to be photographed for printing.

Car card: A poster placed in buses, subways, etc. Also called a Bus card.

Category development index (CDI): A comparison of the percent of sales of a product category in a market to the percent of population in that market.

Channels of distribution: The routes used by a company to distribute its products, e.g., through wholesalers, retailers, mail order, etc.

Chrome: A color photographic transparency.

Circulation: Of a print publication, the average number of copies distributed. For outdoor advertising this refers to the total number of people who have an opportunity to observe a billboard or poster.

Clearance: The process by which media reviews an advertisement for legal, ethical and taste standards, before accepting the ad for publication.

Closing date: The day final copy and other materials must be at the vehicle in order to appear in a specific issue or time slot.

Clutter: When an advertisement is surrounded by an abundance of other ads, thereby forcing it to compete for the viewer's or listener's attention.

Collateral materials: Sales brochures, catalogs, etc.

Color proof: An early full-color print of a finished advertisement, used to evaluate the ad's final appearance.

Color separation: A full-color ad normally is generated through printing four separate colors: yellow, cyan, magenta and black. The color separation consists of four separate screens; one for each of those four colors.

Column inch: A common unit of measurement by newspapers whereby ad space is purchased by the width, in columns, and the depth, in inches. For example, an ad that is three standard columns wide and 5 inches tall (or deep) would be 15 column inches.

Comp layout: A rough layout of an ad with all the elements present.

Consumer advertising: Advertising directed at a person rather than to a business or dealer.

Consumer behavior: Study of how people behave when purchasing and using products and services.

Controlled circulation: Publications, delivered free to readers.

Cooperative (Co-op) program: A system by which ad costs are divided between two or more parties. Usually, such programs are offered by manufacturers to their wholesalers or retailers, as a means of encouraging those parties to advertise the product.

Copy: All spoken words or written text in an advertisement.

Copy testing: Research to determine an ad's effectiveness based on consumer responses to the ad.

Corporate advertising: A campaign that promotes a corporation, rather than a product or service sold by that corporation.

Cost efficiency: For a media schedule, refers to the relative balance of effectively meeting reach and frequency goals at the lowest price.

Cost per inquiry: The cost of getting one person to inquire about a product or service. This is a standard used in direct response advertising.

Cost per rating point (CPP): The cost, per 1 percent of a specified audience, of buying advertising space in a given media vehicle.

Cost per thousand (CPM): The cost, per 1,000 people reached, of buying advertising space in a given media vehicle.

Creative strategy: An outline of what message should be conveyed, to whom and with what tone. This provides the guiding principles for copywriters and art directors who are assigned to develop the advertisement. Within the context of that assignment, any ad that is then created should conform to that strategy.

Creatives: The art directors and copywriters in an ad agency.

Day-after recall test: A research method that tests consumers' memories the day after they have seen an ad, to assess the ad's effectiveness.

Daypart: Broadcast media divide the day into several standard time periods, each of which is called a "daypart." Cost of purchasing advertising time on a vehicle varies by the daypart selected.

Demographic segmentation: Dividing consumers into groups based on selected demographics, so that different groups can be treated differently. For example, two advertisements might be developed, one for adults and one for teenagers, because the two groups are expected to be attracted to different types of advertising appeal.

Demographics: Basic, objective, descriptive classifications of consumers, such as their age, sex, income, education, size of household, ownership of home, etc. This does not include classification by subjective attitudes or opinions of consumers. (See "psychographics" later in Glossary.)

Designated market area (DMA): A geographic designation, used by A.C. Nielsen, which specifies those counties that fall into a specific television market. See also "area of dominant influence."

Direct mail: Marketing communications delivered directly to a prospective buyer in the mail.

Direct marketing: Sending a promotional message directly to consumers, rather than via a mass medium. Includes direct mail and telemarketing.

Direct response: Promotions that permit or request consumers to directly respond to the advertiser by mail, telephone, e-mail or some other means of communication. Some practitioners use this as a synonym for direct marketing.

Distributor: A company or person that distributes a manufacturer's goods to retailers.

Double truck: A two-page spread in a print publication where the ad runs across the middle gutter.

Drive time: Used in radio, this refers to morning and afternoon times when consumers are driving to and from work.

Duplicated audience: That portion of an audience that is reached by more than one media vehicle.

Earned rate: A discounted media rate based on volume or frequency of media placement.

Electric spectacular: Outdoor signs or billboards composed largely of lighting or other electrical components.

End-user: The person who actually uses a product, whether or not they are the one who purchased the product.

Envelope stuffer: A direct mail advertisement included with another mailed message (such as a bill).

Flat rate: A media rate that allows for no discounts.

Flighting: A media schedule involving more advertising at certain time periods and less advertising during other times.

Focus group interview: A research method that brings together a small group of consumers to discuss the product or advertising under the guidance of a trained interviewer.

Font: A typeface style, such as Helvetica, Times Roman, etc., in a single size. A single font includes all 26 letters, along with punctuation, numbers, and other characters.

Four-color process: A printing process that combines differing amounts of each of four colors (red, yellow, blue and black) to provide a full-color print.

Franchised position: An ad position in a periodic publication (e.g., back cover) to which an advertiser is given a permanent or long-term right.

Free-standing insert (FSI): An advertisement or group of ads inserted – but not bound – in a print publication on pages that contain only the ads and are separate from any editorial or entertainment matter.

Frequency: Number of times an average person or home is exposed to a media vehicle (or group of vehicles), within a given time period, usually four weeks.

Fringe time: A time period directly preceding and directly following prime time, on television.

Fulfillment house: A company that receives coupons or refunds and manages their accounting, verification and redemption.

Full-service agency: An advertising firm that handles all aspects of the process, including planning, design, production, and placement. Today, full-service generally suggests that the agency also handles other aspects of marketing communication, such as public relations, sales promotion and direct marketing.

Galley proof: A typeset copy of an ad or editorial material before it is made into pages for final production.

Gatefold: Double or triple-sized pages, generally in magazines, that fold out into a large advertisement.

Guaranteed circulation: A media rate that comes with a guarantee that the publication will achieve a certain circulation.

Generic brand: Products not associated with a private or national brand name.

Gross audience: The audiences of all vehicles or media in a campaign combined.

Gross impressions: Total number of unduplicated people or households represented by a given media schedule.

Gross rating points (GRPs): Reach times average frequency. This is a measure of the advertising weight delivered by a vehicle or vehicles within a given time period.

Halftone: A method of reproducing a black and white photograph or illustration by representing various shades of gray as a series of black and white dots.

House agency: An advertising agency owned and operated by a company (such as Coke, IBM, etc.), as opposed to an independent advertising agency that works for many different client companies.

House organ: A publication owned and operated by an advertiser, used to promote the advertiser's products or services.

Households using television (HUT): The number of households in a given market watching television at a certain time. This term is used by A.C. Nielsen.

ID: Station identification during a commercial break in a television or radio program.

Image advertising: Promoting the image, or general perception, of a product or service. Used for differentiating brands of parity products.

Imprinted product: A promotional product. This is a product with a company logo or advertising message printed on it.

In-pack premium: A gift or sample included in the packaging of another product

Insert: An advertisement, collection of advertisements or other promotional matter published by an advertiser or group of advertisers to be inserted into a magazine or newspaper. It may be bound into the publication, or inserted without binding.

Insertion: Refers to putting an ad in a print publication.

Insertion order: This is essentially the written order/receipt for advertising in print media. It represents an agency or advertiser's authorization for a publisher to run a specific ad in a specific print publication on a certain date at a specified price.

Institutional advertising: Advertising to promote an organization rather than a product or service in order to create public support and goodwill.

Integrated Marketing Communication (IMC): A management concept designed to make all aspects of marketing communication (e.g., advertising, sales promotion, public relations and direct marketing) work together as a unified force, rather than permitting each to work in isolation.

Island display: An in-store product display positioned away from competing products, typically in the middle or at the end of an aisle.

Island position: A print ad that is completely surrounded by editorial material, or a broadcast ad surrounded by program content, with no adjoining advertisements to compete for audience attention.

Jingle: A short song, usually mentioning a brand or product benefit, used in a commercial.

Kerning: Spacing between the letters of a word.

Layout: A drawing indicating the relative positions of the elements of an ad.

Leading: The space between lines of type.

Leave-behind: A premium left with prospective customers by a salesperson to remind them of the product or service being sold.

Letterpress: A printing method that stamps ink onto paper using raised lettering.

Lifestyle segmentation: Separating consumers into groups, based on their hobbies, interests, and other aspects of their lifestyles.

Local advertising: (1) Advertising to a local merchant or business as opposed to regional or national advertising. (2) Advertising placed at rates available to local merchants.

Local rate: An advertising rate charged to a local advertiser, typically a retailer, by local media and publications, as distinguished from a national rate that is charged to a national advertiser, typically a manufacturer.

Logotype (logo): A brand name, publication title or the like, presented in a special lettering style or typeface and used like a trademark.

Loss leader: A retail item advertised at an invitingly low price in order to attract customers for the purchase of other, more profitable merchandise.

Macromarketing: A type of marketing in which a company adapts itself to uncontrollable factors within the industry.

Mail-in premium: A premium obtained by mailing in a suitable response to the manufacturer or distributor, with or without money.

Mail-order advertising: Advertising that supplies paperwork for the purpose of soliciting a purchase made through the mail.

Make good: (1) To present a commercial announcement after its scheduled time due to an error. (2) To rerun a commercial announcement because of technical difficulties the previous time it was run. (3) To rerun a print advertisement due to similar circumstances.

Market profile: A summary of the characteristics of a market including information of typical purchasers and competitors, and often general information on the economy and retailing patterns of an area.

Market segmentation: Dividing a market by a strategy directed at gaining a major portion of sales to a subgroup of a category, rather than a more limited share of purchases by all category users.

Market share: The percentage of a product category's sales, in terms of dollars or units, obtained by a brand, line or company.

Marketing firm: A business that affects the distribution and sales of goods and services from producer to consumer; including products or service development, pricing, packaging, advertising, merchandising and distribution.

Marketing mix: All of a product's or service's marketing efforts, including product features, pricing, packaging, advertising, merchandising, distribution and marketing budget.

Marketing research: The gathering, recording, analyzing and use of data relating to the transfer and sale of goods and services from producer to consumer.

Master tape: An edited audio tape or video tape used for dubs.

Mechanical (paste-up): A finished layout photographed for offset printing.

Media buying service: An agency specializing in media buying services.

Media concentration theory: The technique of scheduling media that involves buying space in one medium only and developing strength through concentration.

Media plan: A scheme designed to select the proper demographics for an advertising campaign through efficient and effective media selection.

Media strategy: A plan of action for bringing advertising messages to the attention of consumers through the use of appropriate media.

Medium (plural, Media): A vehicle or group of vehicles used to convey information, news, entertainment and advertising messages to an audience. These include television, cable television, magazines, radio, billboards, etc.

NAB: National Association of Broadcasters. An association whose membership is largely composed of radio and television stations.

NARB: National Advertising Review Board of the Council of Better Business Bureaus. When an alleged problem arises with an advertisement, and a satisfactory solution is not obtained via the NAD, described above, the NARB acts in the capacity of an appeals board, reviewing the NAD's decision and passing judgment on it.

Narrowcasting: Using a broadcast medium to appeal to audiences with special interests.

National advertising: Advertising aimed at a national market, as opposed to local advertising.

National brand: A nationally distributed brand name product.

Near-pack (Near Pack Premium): An item offered free or at a discount with the purchase of another product.

Negative: Developed film that containing an image that has reversed shadows and light areas.

Network: A national or regional group of affiliated broadcast stations contractually bound to distribute radio or television programs for simultaneous transmission.

Nielsen rating: A measurement of the percentage of U.S. television households tuned to a network program for a minute of its telecast.

O&O (owend and operated) station: A radio or television station owned and operated by a network.

Opticals: Visual effects used to instill interest as well as portray mood and continuity to a commercial. Dissolves, cross fades, and montages are all opticals.

Out-of-home advertising: Exposure to advertising and mass media away from one's home. Included are outdoor, point-of-purchase and radio.

Outdoor advertising: Any outdoor sign that publicly promotes a product or service, such as billboards, movie kiosks, etc.

Package insert: Advertising material included in merchandise packages that advertises goods, services, or offers financial incentives (coupons) for purchase.

Painted bulletin: A freestanding steel or wooden structure, which bears a hand painted copy message.

Panels: Regular and illuminated types of outdoor advertising.

Pantone Matching System (PMS): A system that precisely characterizes a color, so that a color can be matched, even by different printers. By knowing the Pantone color specifications, a printer does not even need to see a sample of the color in order to match it.

Parity products: Product categories where the several brands within possess functionally equivalent attributes, making one brand a satisfactory substitute for most other brands in that category.

Pass-along readers: A reader who becomes familiar with a publication without the purchase of a publication. These readers are taken into account when calculating the total number of readers of a publication.

Photoanimation: A process of creating animation through the use of still photographs.

Photoboards: A set of still photographs made from a television commercial, accompanied with a script, to be kept as records by an agency or client.

Photoengraving: (1) The process of making letterpress printing plates through photochemical means. (2) A picture printed from a plate made by this process.

Photostat: A type of high contrast photographic negative or positive in the form of paper. Also referred to as Stat.

Pica: (1) A unit of measurement for type specification and printing measureing width; 6 picas to one inch. (2) A size of type, 12 points.

Piggyback: (1) A direct mail offer included free with another offer. (2) Two commercials shown back-to-back by the same sponsor.

Point: Point-of-Purchase (POP) displays. Advertising display material located at the retail store, usually placed in an area where payment is made, such as a check-out counter.

Poster panel: An outdoor billboard on which advertising is displayed on printed paper sheets rather than painted.

Posttesting Testing the effects of an ad after it has appeared in the media.

Preferred position: Placement in a printed publication thought to attract most reader attention and sold at a higher rate; for example, the back cover of a magazine.

Premium: An item, other than the product itself, which is offered free or at a nominal price as an incentive to purchase the advertised product or service.

Pretesting: Testing an advertisement or an audience sample prior to placing the ad in the media.

Prime time: The broadcast periods viewed or listened to by the greatest number of persons and for which a station charges the most for air time. In television, the hours are usually 8 p.m. to 11 p.m. EST (7 p.m. to 10 p.m. CST).

Private brand: Product brand owned by a retailer, wholesaler, dealer or merchant, as opposed to a manufacturer or producer, and bearing its own company name or another name it owns exclusively. Also referred to as private label.

Product differentiation: Developing unique product differences intending to influence demand.

Product life cycle: A marketing theory in which products or brands follow a sequence of stages, including: introduction, growth, maturity and sales decline.

Product management: Assigning specific products or brands to be handled by single managers within an advertising agency.

Product positioning: The consumer perception of a product or service as compared to its competition.

Product-related segmentation: A method of identifying consumers through the amount of product usage, usually categorized demographically or psychographically.

Production: Process of physically preparing the advertising idea for a print or broadcast advertisement.

Progressive proofs (Progs): Set of proofs made during the four-color printing process showing each color plate separately and in combination. Also referred to as color proofs.

Promotion: All forms of communication, other than advertising, that call attention to products and services by adding extra values the purchase. Includes temporary discounts, allowances, premium offers, coupons, contests, sweepstakes, etc.

Proof: An preview print used for the purpose of checking the correctness and quality of the material to be printed.

Psychographics: A term that describes consumers or audience members on the basis of psychological characteristics, initially determined by standardized tests.

Public relations (PR): Communication with various sectors of the public to influence their attitudes and opinions in the interest of promoting a person, product, or idea.

Public relations advertising: Advertising by a corporation that focuses on public interest but maintains a relationship to the corporation's products or agencies.

Public service advertising (PSA): Advertising with a central focus on public welfare, generally sponsored by a nonprofit institution, civic group, religious organization, trade association or political group.

Psychological segmentation: The separation of consumers into psychological characteristic categories on the basis of standardized tests.

Qualitative research: A method of advertising research that emphasizes the quality of awareness in consumer perceptions and attitudes; for example, in-depth interviews and focus groups.

Quantitative research: A method of advertising research that emphasizes incidence of consumer trends measurement within a population.

Random sample: A sample taken from any given population in which each person maintains equal chances of selection.

Rate: (1) The amount charged by a communications medium to an advertiser based on unit of space or time purchased. The rate may vary from national to local campaigns, or may be fixed. (2) To estimate a particular media's audience size based on a research sample.

Rate card: Information cards, provided by both print and broadcast media, which contain information concerning advertising costs, mechanical requirements, issue dates, closing dates, cancellation dates and circulation data, etc.

Rating point: (1) In television, 1 percent of all TV households who are viewing a particular station at a given time. (2) In radio, 1 percent of all listeners who are listening to a particular station at a given time. Both instances vary depending on time of day.

Reach: (1) The estimated number of individuals in the audience of a broadcast who are reached at least once during a specific period of time. (2) Also applies to out-of-home advertising audiences.

Readership: (1) The total number of a publication's readers (includes primary and pass-along readers). (2) The percentage of people that can recall a particular advertisement, aided or unaided.

Residuals: A sum paid to a performer on a TV or radio commercial each time it is run, and is usually established by AFTRA (American Federation of Television and Radio Artists) or SAG (Screen Actors Guild) contracts.

Retail advertising: Advertising that promotes local merchandisers' goods and services. Also referred to as local advertising.

Retouching: To alter photographs, artwork or film to emphasize or introduce desired features and to eliminate unwanted ones.

Road block: A method of scheduling broadcast commercials to obtain maximum reach by simultaneously showing the identical advertisement on several different stations.

Rough: An unfinished layout of an ad that shows only a general conception.

Rough cut: A preliminary arrangement of film or tape shots roughly edited together without voiceover or music in the early stages of editing.

Run-of-press (ROP): A newspaper publisher's option to place an ad anywhere in the publication that they choose, as opposed to preferred position. Also referred to as run-of-paper.

Run-of-schedule (ROS): A station's option to place a commercial in any time slot that they choose.

Rushes: Rough, unedited prints of a commercial to be used for editing purposes. Also referred to as dallies.

Sales promotion: Marketing activities that stimulate consumer purchasing and dealer effectiveness through a combination of personal selling, advertising and all supplementary selling activities.

Seasonality: The variation in sales for goods and services throughout the year, depending on the season, e.g. hot chocolate is advertised more in the winter, as opposed to summer months.

Self-liquidating premium: A premium offer paid by the consumer whose total cost, including handling fees, are paid for in the basic sales transaction.

Self-mailer: A direct-mail piece in which no envelope or wrapper is required for mailing.

Semi-liquidator: A premium offer that is partially paid by the consumer as well as the manufacturer.

Sets in use (SIU): The percent of television sets that are tuned into a particular broadcast during a specific amount of time.

Share-of-audience: The percent of audiences that are tuned into a particular medium at a given time, e.g. the number of people watching television between the hours of 8 p.m. to 11 p.m.

Shelf screamers (shelf talkers): A printed advertising message which is hung over the edge of a retail store shelf, e.g., "On Special," or "SaleItem."

Silk screening: A color printing method in which ink is forced through a stencil placed over a screen that blocks out areas of an image, and onto the printing surface. Also referred to as serigraphy.

Simmons Market Research Bureau (SMRB): A syndicated service that provides audience exposure and product usage data for print and broadcast media.

Slicks: A high-quality proof of an advertisement printed on glossy paper which is suited for reproduction.

Slotting allowances: Fees paid by a manufacturer to a retailer for the retailer's shelf space.

Split run: Two or more different forms of an advertisement that are run simultaneously in different copies of the same publication, used to test the effectiveness of one advertisement over another (to appeal to regional or other specific markets).

Spot announcements: Commercial or public service announcements that are placed on television or radio programs.

Spot television (or radio): Time slots in geographic broadcast areas, purchased on a market-to-market basis rather than through a network.

Spread: Refers to a pair of facing pages in a periodical, or an advertisement that is printed across two such pages.

Staggered schedule: A schedule of advertisements in a number of periodicals that have different insertion dates.

Standard Industrial Classification (SIC): Defined by the U.S. Department of Commerce to be a classification of businesses in a numeric hierarchy.

Standard Rate and Data Service (SRDS): A commercial firm that publishes reference volumes including up-to-date information on rates, requirements, closing dates and other information necessary for ad placement in the media.

Starch scores: A result of a method used by Daniel Starch and staff in their studies of advertising readership, which include "noted" (the percent of readers who viewed the tested ad), "associated" (the percent of readers who associated the ad with the advertiser), and "read-most" (the percent of readers who read half or more of the copy).

Starch Readership Service: A research organization (Starch INRA Hooper) that provides an advertisement's rank in issue and Starch scores.

Storyboard: A blueprint for a TV commercial that is drawn to portray copy, dialogue and action with caption notes regarding filming, audio components and script.

Strategic planning: Determination of the steps required to achieve the optimum fit between the organization and the marketplace.

Superimposition (super): A process in TV production where an image, words or phrases are imposed over another image.

Supplementary media: Non-mass media vehicles that are used to promote products, e.g., point-of-purchase advertising.

Supplier: Companies that sell goods or services to an advertising agency for use in constructing advertisements, e.g., design studios, color houses, printers and paper producers.

Sweeps: Refers to a period of time during the months of November, February and May, when both Nielson and Arbitron survey all local market broadcast media for the purpose of rating the stations and their programming.

Syndicated program: A television or radio program that is distributed in more than one market by an organization other than a network.

Tabloid: A type of newspaper that is roughly half the size of a standard newspaper.

Tag line: A slogan or phrase that visually conveys the most important product attribute or benefit the advertiser wishes to convey. Generally, a theme to a campaign.

Target audience: A specified audience or demographic group for which an advertising message is designed

Target market: A group of individuals, whom, collectively, are the intended recipients of an advertiser's message.

Tear sheets: A page cut from a magazine or newspaper that is sent to the advertiser as proof of the ad insertion. Also used to check color reproduction of advertisements.

Teaser campaign: An advertising campaign aimed at arousing interest and curiosity for a product.

Thumbnail: A rough, simple, often small sketch used to show the basic layout of an ad.

Tracking studies: A type of research study that follows the same group of subjects over an extended period of time.

Trade advertising: Advertising designed to increase sales specifically for retailers and wholesalers.

Trade name: The name under which a company operates.

Trademark: Icon, symbol or brand name used to identify a specific manufacturer, product or service.

Traffic builder: A promotional tactic using direct mail. Designed to draw consumers to the mailer's location.

Transit advertising: Advertising that appears on public transportation or on waiting areas and bus stops.

Transparency: A positive color photographic image on clear film.

Transparent ink: Ink used in four-color printing process that allows for colors underneath the ink to show through.

Trim size: A size of a magazine or newspaper page after trimming.

Turnover: The rate of audience change for a specific program during a specific amount of time.

Type font: Refers to the complete alphabet for a specific typeface.

Typeface: A designed alphabet with consistent characteristics and attributes.

Typography: The designated setting of type for printing purposes.

Unaided recall: A research method in which a respondent is given no assistance in answering questions regarding a specific advertisement.

Unique selling proposition: The unique product benefit that the competition can not claim.

Up-front buys: The purchasing of both broadcast and print early in the buying season.

Values and lifestyles (VALS) research: A research method that psychologically groups consumers based on certain characteristics such as their values, lifestyles and demographics.

Vehicle: A specific channel or publication for carrying the advertising message to a target audience. For example, one medium would be magazines, while one vehicle would be *Time* magazine.

Velox: A type of paper used for its superior reproduction qualities.

Vertical publications: Publications whose editorial content deals with the interests of a specific industry, e.g., *National Petroleum Magazine* and *Retail Baking Today*.

Vignette: (1) An illustration that has soft edges, often produced using cutouts or masks. (2) A photograph or halftone in which the edges, or parts of, are shaded off to a very light gray.

Voiceover (VO): The technique of using the voice of an unseen speaker during film, slides or other voice material.

Wash drawings: Tonal drawing, similar to watercolor, intended for halftone reproduction.

Waste circulation: (1) Advertising in an area where the product or service is not available or has no sales potential. (2) People in an advertiser's audience who are not potential consumers.

Wear out: The point when an advertising campaign loses its effectiveness due to repeated ad overplay.

Wipe: A transition of scenes in a visual production where one image appears to wipe the previous one from the screen.

About the Author

Ira Berkowitz is an advertising executive with over 25 years of experience in the industry. He is the former senior vice president of Ogilvy & Mather and president of Grey Advertising's Beaumont Bennett, and current president of Involvement Marketing Inc., a consultancy devoted to building brands.